ON KARL MARX

Azimuth defines direction by generating an arc between a fixed point and a variable, between the determined truths of the past and the unknown data of the future.

ON KARL MARX

ERNST BLOCH

AN *AZIMUTH* BOOK
HERDER AND HERDER

1971
HERDER AND HERDER NEW YORK
232 Madison Avenue, New York 10016

Original edition: *Über Karl Marx,* © 1968 by Suhrkamp Verlag;
from *Das Prinzip Hoffnung,* 3 vols. *(passim),* © 1959, Suhrkamp
Verlag, Frankfurt am Main.

Translated by John Maxwell.

CONTENTS

ON KARL MARX

MARX AS A STUDENT

True growth is always open and youthful, and youth implies growth. Youth, like growth, is restless; growth, like youth, would lay the future open in the present. Apathy is their common enemy, and they are allies in the fight for that which has never been but is now coming into its own. Now is its day; and its day is as young and as vital as those who proclaim it and keep faith with it.

If we look back to the very dawn of our daytime, we look back to the young Marx in his first years of intellectual ferment. What we can learn of one who was surely the most passionately alert of all students is encouraging, and a challenge to us, the heirs of his maturity. We still have a letter of November 1837 that the nineteen-year-old Karl wrote to his father—who lived in the same town as Jenny von Westphalen, his son's future wife. But this letter addressed to "Dearest Father" does not merely throw light on the relations between Dr. Heinrich Marx and his famous son: its fresh and creative spirit makes it a living document for every young student. Of course, this is a vivacity characteristic of the letters of great writers in their youth (one thinks of Goethe in Leipzig and Strasbourg, of Byron, of Georg Büchner). But here one can sense the ardor of the great *thinker* to come. Even though Jenny gives occasion for a more lyrical note, this is a letter without equal as a record of a young philosopher's tempestuous and far-ranging mind.

The young man's every experience is heightened: "The rocks could not be sharper than my sensibility . . . and art itself could not match Jenny's beauty." Everything he sees is rich with significance, yet everything is ready to change and make room for something new in the wind. "Every metamorphosis," writes this student whose maturity would be so meaningful for the world's future, "is partly a swan song and partly the overture to a great new poem which, in a medley of blurred though brilliant colors, is still struggling to emerge as form." Marx responds to a world in the process of development; to a summons and to a melody; to that which comes into being and then must pass away. Yet he checks any tendency to dream vaguely of the future; all the anticipation of a Marx-in-becoming moves him to engage in an insatiable though exacting tussle with the scholars: with law and philosophy. This is Marx as a young Faust—not Goethe's, but the flesh-and-blood Faust proper to the age. Three and a half years were to pass before he submitted his doctoral dissertation, and the Marx of this letter is neither the pure idealist of his poems nor a skeptic. His approach is already essentially logical and scientific, and, rather than follow the Mephistophelean counsel to "despise reason and knowledge," he is filled with enthusiasm for these doors of entry to the world. The shape the future will take, its actuality, is being established in the ferment of the present; out of subjectivity and abstraction must emerge the face of concrete reality—the thing that really matters. The only obstructions are the mists of false consciousness and abstract thought, both of which Marx rejects—together with Hegel, and against him: "In the concrete expression of a living world of ideas, such as law, the State, Nature, and philosophy as a whole, the object itself must be observed as it develops. There must be no arbitrary categorizations: the rationale of the thing itself must proceed in its own course of internal con-

10

tradiction and so attain to its own intrinsic unity." Mind is still the agent, but the perception of the later Marx is already apparent in the inversion—the "standing on its feet"—of the *ratio* of the thing.

Obviously the writer of this letter is not wrapped up in himself. Though his quest for knowledge is no uniform, untroubled process, but one which has known blind alleys and moments of obscurity, it is always undertaken anew, moves ever onwards. Marx describes the quantity of writing he has done: poems, a vast opus on the philosophy of law, a dialogue, notes, notes, notes; manuscripts which ended in anguish or self-reproach; and his voracious reading and expeditions across and straight through the *globus intellectualis;* yet all related with the eagerness of an explorer in virgin lands. This optimism contrasts remarkably with the merely imitative intellectual spirit predominant in post-Hegelian Berlin—a twilight feeling, as if somehow nothing really impressive could be produced after Hegel, by whom the world had been thoroughly schematized; as if the "world spirit" had arrived philosophically in Hegel's teaching, and all that was left for young philosophers was to transplant it from its initial Berlin residence to the left, or subjective and "critical," side of "self-consciousness." The stirrings of the 1848 revolution were not felt in this environment, and were not produced by an idealism which the left Hegelians had endowed with a spurious rigor and clarity. The opposed wretchedness of the period before the March Revolution of 1848 was only increased by an apathy which was unopposable on an idealistic basis—an intellectual decadence which continued to affect the entire prescriptive philosophy of the nineteenth century, apart from Marxism.

The most obviously unique characteristic of the young Marx was his objective and youthful vigor amid the surrounding post-Hegelian decay. The young philosopher was concerned essentially neither with himself nor with the insipid flatlands about him; instead he reflected the light of a world that had not yet come to be but on whose horizon he stood. The letter of

11

1837 and the doctoral dissertation of 1841 are wholly free of the lethargy of idealism; and more than a knowledge of Feuerbach enabled their author to see the era not as one of mellow decay but as a turning point—a material turning point, with Marx as the discoverer of the new. Hence the wholly *public* self-consciousness of the young Marx: a self-awareness concerned with the actuality of the future as the future of actuality. His genius accorded with the revolutionary mandate of the age; the subjective and objective suasions to shape the future were allied. Rosenkranz, a contemporary Hegelian, offered a formulation in his *Psychology* (1843) that found its living exponent in Marx: "The characteristic quality of genius is not, like that of talent, a formal versatility (even though it can enjoy that too), but a realization of what is objectively necessary in a certain sphere as its individual destiny. Accordingly, a man of genius is properly exercised only in the development of *history,* for he must pass directly beyond everything that is merely given, as it is, and obtain as personal gratification that which, according to the objective process of the matter, is really timely. He prevails with a daemonic force in the accomplishment of this task; apart from it he is powerless, and despite his undoubted versatility in the acquisition of knowledge can achieve nothing really new." Of course, "personal gratification" did not apply to the young Marx; he went beyond the implications of this bourgeois term in being moved by objective optimism—a mutual illumination in which no distinction might be made between the individual and his task. The student's letter and the dissertation offer fore-glimpses of what Marx was to write not so long after—in 1843: "Just as philosophy discovers its material weapons in the proletariat, so the proletariat discovers its intellectual weapons in philosophy" (Introduction to *A Contribution to the Critique of Hegel's Philosophy of Right*). No longer overawed by his mentor, Marx took what was living in Hegel's philosophy, and became his true heir in making the proletariat's right to inherit the earth his prime concern.

And so the young Marx asserted his youthful spirit and

12

affirmed its true value. He was not one of the many famous young men who have been lauded for their retreat into the self, into the world-weariness of the solitary guardian of a precious inner flame. Nor did he practice a stoic aloofness from the affairs of the world, but dismissed such an attitude as tantamount to the behavior of the moth which, "when the universal sun has gone down, seeks the lamplight of a private world." Least of all was the apprentice dialectician lacking in a sense of history, conceived as mediation and transition. For he begins his letter (and remember that he was only nineteen) with a retrospective survey that is also an anticipation of the new, of an action and achievement as yet unknown: "There are moments in life that seem to mark the end of a certain period, but also clearly indicate a new direction. At such transitional points we feel compelled to examine past and present with the eagle eye of the mind in order to understand our real situation. Indeed, world history itself favors this kind of survey and self-reflection, which often makes it seem to go backward or to stand still, whereas in fact it is throwing itself into an armchair in order to comprehend its own achievement—the action of the spirit." *Action* is in question; ultimately, the historical sense tends toward action, and does not swamp but nurtures it; does not drag the vessel of achievement down into the vastness of history, but carries it forward upon its waters.

Whenever he looks back from the healthful repose of his armchair (but a captain's chair, drawn up to the chart table), Marx is always at work with a sextant, in order to estimate the latitude and longitude of the social voyage his age and he, he and his age, are making together. In the preparatory work for his dissertation he uses a splendidly apt illustration from Greek history to emphasize the importance of *what is to be done:* the task ahead after the stocktaking, after the idealism. What is wanted is not a mere imitative patching up or a realization of idealistic philosophy without its transcendence. Instead Marx says: "In such times, half-hearted spirits are like brave generals in reverse; they think that they can repair the damage by

13

reducing their forces, by dispersal, by making an armistice with the demands that necessity now appears to impose upon them. Whereas Themistocles, when Athens was threatened with destruction, persuaded its citizens to leave it altogether, and to take to sea and found a new Athens on a new element." For Marx, this new Athens was no longer the mere statement of the contradiction between the wretched apathy of the German condition and a sublimity which just made the world seem all the more hopelessly lacerated the more philosophy as a whole was put above or even side by side with it. The new Athens appeared instead in the form of praxis: as theoretical action that knows what it wants; as revolutionary action that wants what it knows.

As Marx says in the dissertation itself: "It is a law of psychology that the theoretical spirit which has become intrinsically free turns into practical energy, and, as *will,* emerges from a shadowy existence . . . to oppose the reality which exists outside it . . . It is *criticism* that measures the individual existence against the essence, and the specific reality against the idea. But this *direct realization* of philosophy, in accordance with its innermost nature, is charged with contradictions; and this essential nature emerges as the external appearance on which it sets its own stamp."

It was not long before the political experience of the editorship of the *Rheinische Zeitung,* and the initial discovery of social reality as economic reality, allowed Marx to see the "contradictions" as existing primarily in the *reality* of capitalism and only consequently, secondarily, in philosophy. And he acknowledged "criticism" as the kind that sets reality, featuring the unresolved contradiction, primarily against itself. "Hence the critic," as Marx wrote to Arnold Ruge in September 1843, "can develop the true reality from the *inherent* forms of existing reality as its proper intention and ultimate aim." Eventually, the mature Marx was to reveal the "true reality" as that of the particular productive forces and conditions of production, and the "intention" as that of the social tendency. But Marx the student had already abandoned the old Athens, or the idealistic philosophy of self-contemplative thought. The new was none other than the real Athens, retaining the inheritance of classical philosophy, but established "on another element." This new Athens would subsequently become the realm of the real freedom of the future, whose power and glory would not be dependent on a slave economy: in this way alone would it be the Athens of truly humane learning.

True growth is always open and youthful. Once again that which is coming into its own is objective as well as subjective youth. This new element is no longer in the stage of conception but already in the process of construction, despite the inertia, stupidity, and bloody countenance of an evanescent world. Ultimately, those young men and women who are truly youthful feel an affinity not only with the young but with the mature Marx: they are shoots on the tree of Marxist-Leninism, which would wither if it did not bear blossom and fruit at one and the same time. The mature Marx, that great *worker,* is the truth of the young Marx, for he put his plan into action, and turned his knowledge into operating instructions. "To few is it given," cried the young Goethe as he stood before Strashourg Cathedral, "actually to body forth on a precise and majestic scale the towering conception of the spirit within." But it is given to all to spread such an idea—the human structure of Marxism—as reality on the face of this earth; to make it reach ever higher into an unalienated and ever more truly human realm. And young people precisely are called to this chief end: to fulfill the true humanization of man wherever it cries out for fulfillment and thrills their spirit with its will to be.

15

KARL MARX AND HUMANITY: THE MATERIAL OF HOPE

It is not true that the shortest line is always the straightest.

LESSING

It is not enough to represent things as they are, but it is necessary to think of what is desired and what is possible.

GORKI

The great truth of our age (knowledge of this alone is not enough, yet without such knowledge no truth of any significance can be ascertained) is that our earth is sinking into barbarism, because the relations of ownership are being forcibly held down to the means of production.

BRECHT

The Authentic Artisan

No man has been satisfied by desire alone. Wishing is not only ineffectual but enervates if what is wished is not willed, and

16

willed resolutely. It must be accompanied, too, by a keen far-seeing vision which shows the will what can be done. But ultimately all this does not make the mere individual take his so-called personal concerns less seriously, less like the petite bourgeoisie who see no farther than their noses, nor desire to do so. The man who is just so *narrow* may even feel himself to be a participant in events of common concern so long as and to the degree that they concern him for the time being. But once this is settled, the all too private individual withdraws anew into his own affairs until some later day. He puts the cards of the common good (which he sees as something quite external to him) on the table and calls it a day.

But this type would not be as he is but for his counterpart, the completely *busy type*—however he may actually oppose the cause, which does not mean only in a bourgeois, despiritualized, and reified form. In this case it is not just that his individual being hides away in a small restricted wigwam, in a Philistine or even snobbish way, and then decays in very privacy; rather, his individual existence dissolves into wholly external relationships, and ends in a merely technical velocity—which may occasionally serve public ends. However, because there is hardly anything personal, humane, or expressive here, but for the most part only native or factitious nullity, very little that is really useful emerges. For the value of a group is generally no greater than the individuals who go to make it up, and busywork, in which no one is really moving, becomes mere repetition and finally stagnation. Zeros, whether voluntary or coerced, add up to zero; and mud when trodden on just oozes, but does not harden.

The worst situation in this regard exists when half a group has gone red and the other half has stayed petit bourgeois— and this latter half continues to transmit, foster, and develop all the noble values of the bourgeois Philistine. Then not only the love for some tangible kitsch is present but, even more lamentably, the production of human kitsch and the degeneration of human relationships in the very midst of an ascent to the freest and most courageous goals. In such cases the path forward is not blocked, but made difficult and artificially prevented from remaining as fresh as it properly is, and as widely attractive. Therefore the trained, the authentic, artisans of our happiness have to bestir themselves without losing themselves; yet they must carry out their tasks with so much common will and vision that their own achievement does not remain an individual and all too private affair. Then both struggle and assistance will proceed effectively, and there will be no mere restriction or empty achievement. For aid and liberation must have a human face; and a human face must be able to smile.

"To Abrogate All Relationships in which Man Is Degraded, Enslaved, Abandoned, and Wretched"

What has brought to the red flag those who did not, in a sense, need it? Perhaps that sympathetic movement of the heart (insofar as it exists at all) before such universal suffering. Perhaps the conscience which this misery awakens in some silent members of the ruling class while their active business partners pocket the profits quite undisturbed. And perhaps the thirst for knowledge also helped by providing in scientific analysis a knife to lop off the branch on which a young man or woman of solid circumstances and expectations had been sitting. Of course, one hardly comes by this sort of knowledge without some previous ethical interest in obtaining it; if knowledge has been arrived at only by contemplation and has remained at this level, one will scarcely draw any actual, revolutionary conclusions. For example, Sombart once said he was highly embarrassed when people asked him if he was a socialist. The question was quite ambiguous: it could refer either to what was subjectively desirable, or to what was objectively inevitable, in socialism. In the latter case, Sombart, through scientific insight, was (alas!) a socialist; in the former, on the other hand, when the question was put as to his position, being bourgeois he was wholly anti-red. *Quod erat demonstrandum*—and very definitely shown forth in Sombart. On the other hand, the above mentioned sentiment, along with conscience and attitude, are not always enough to engender class treason against the well-to-do. Marx himself expressed in a circular letter his opposition to a certain Hermann Kriege, who undertook to combat misery on the basis of love alone, and so ultimately as if out of philanthropic condescension from above. Marx also opposed those who had set Kriege thinking in this way—that is, the "dew of sentiment suffused with love," which he found not only among the "German socialists" but in many humanitarian passages in Ludwig Feuerbach's writings. Feuerbach did indeed remain aloof from the socialist movement, and even from the 1848 revolution, although in his later years he avowed an affiliation with the workers' party.

Hence the least that is required is a *collaboration* of feeling, conscience, and above all knowledge, in order to present a socialist consciousness in opposition to one's own past social being, with the significant and contrasting result that one's consciousness can no longer be permitted to correspond to the social nature one had possessed for so long. The result in certain areas would be the condition described, and defined *objectively,* not just psychologically, in the *Communist Manifesto:* "Finally, in periods when the class struggle nears the decisive hour, the process of dissolution going on within the ruling class, in fact within the whole range of the old society, assumes such a violent, glaring character, that a small section of the ruling class cuts itself adrift, and joins the revolutionary class, the class that holds the future in its hands." With this threatened defection of the foremost younger intellectuals from their class, with so peculiar a mixture of a backward glance at the ruins, a look into the future, and humanitarianism, a defensive countermovement begins to develop. The strongest manifestation of this kind was fascism, but long before then there were finer misty adumbrations of it, which then became apparent about it, and have arisen once more in

19

its aftermath. All such countermovements are motivated by an impulse to divert, in a reactionary fashion, any who might be inclined to follow the socialist line.

When it became clear that Marx could not be kept quiet despite every effort, then he had to be greatly fined down, and above all, *incredibile dictu,* to be de-revolutionized. Hence he has been represented as a poor relation of Kierkegaard or Pascal, in which case a sort of pietist. Accordingly, as a consistent outcome of the furling of the red flag, one Knittermeyer, an existentialist, maintains that it would not be "just" to Marx to saddle him with what today appears under the name of communist ideology. Even Heidegger, in that *lucus a non lucendo* of his which bears the title *A Letter on Humanism,* was able to patronize (at least in the period of denazification) an emasculated and decapitated Marx figure, which in spite of—or because of—its lack of correspondence with the real Marx, proved the more acceptable. But this goes to show that the combination of feeling, conscience, and objective insight that so often has caused intellectuals to move to the left makes Marx indispensable. Clearly Marx unadulterated offers a secure paradigm of the red path of the intellect: the model of a humanism that conceives itself in action. This found expression in Marx early on as a distinctive concern with no element of softness. First, this acute and sensitive man was aware of his own humanity; secondly, others with the same human countenance were being treated like dogs. No mercy could be spared for those who treated them in this way; on the contrary, to tolerate the oppressors would really be inhuman in regard to the oppressed and humiliated. The "fake goodness" (as Münzer termed Luther's intervention on behalf of the overlords) which condemns all violence unless exerted by the exploiters is far removed from Marx. Equally remote is that inauthentic pacifism which, since Marx, has been a feature of a gelatinous indiscriminate forgiveness that allows no decisions which might be completely burdensome to a partially conquered master class—as was the case in 1918, and certainly in 1945.

20

Instead, the humanitarianism of Marx was not general and abstract but personally *addressed* and directed to those who alone needed it. Like Münzer, Marx took up the whip with which Jesus had driven the money changers from the temple. Therefore, his humanitarianism, precisely because it is concrete depending on the direction in which it faces, simultaneously manifests a pervasive indignation, while calling men to action and seeking, finding and proclaiming their objective redemption.

Even in regard to misery Marx sees more than just misery, unlike all the abstract sympathizers and especially the abstract utopians. For him, the explosive factor in poverty really becomes a dynamic, explosive force, directed against the cause of that misery, which, once it realizes its causes, itself becomes the lever of revolution. The humanitarianism of Marx, as directed to the least of his brethren, proves itself in his endeavor to understand from their roots the degradation and induced nullity of most of his brethren, in order to attack their very roots. The zero point of the most extreme alienation, as represented by the proletariat, ultimately becomes the point of dialectical reversal. Within the nothingness of this zero point, Marx teaches, we may find our whole world. Consequently, the alienation, dehumanization, and objectification, the transformation of all people and things into commodities, which capitalism increasingly has brought about, comprise for Marx the ancient enemy which in capitalism as capitalism has finally achieved a victory beyond anything in the past. Certainly humanism is the born enemy of this dehumanization. Indeed, since Marxism is essentially only this struggle against the dehumanization which reaches its acme in capitalism (until the latter is utterly transcended), it follows *e contrario* that true Marxism, in its dynamics of the class struggle, and in its substantive goal, is, and must be, humanism and humanitarianism enhanced. Above all, the various adulterations of and deviations from humanism can be validly criticized or transcended only from within Marxism. For Marxism alone is the heir of whatever was intended by the earlier revolutionary

21

bourgeoisie in respect of human decency. And only Marxism, by reason of its knowledge that class society, especially the capitalist type, is responsible for every variety of self-alienation, has penetrated to its roots, which *can* be removed. As the eliminative power of the proletariat increases, so the circle of those drawn to Marxist humanitarianism widens, and this real humanism then reaches beyond the radically exploited to *all who suffer in common under capitalism.* The cardinal humanistic elements in the social revolution will finally remove the darkness of self-alienation from all mankind, or, as Marx says in his Introduction to *A Critique of the Hegelian Philosophy of Right:* "The criticism of religion ends with the doctrine that *man* is the highest being for man, and hence with the categorical imperative to overthrow all conditions in which man is a degraded, enslaved, abandoned, and wretched creature . . ."

This material "categorical imperative" is by no means, as alleged by the bisectors of Marx, confined to the young Marx. No part of it.was suppressed when Marx transferred what he had formerly termed "real humanism" into the materialist philosophy of history. Even in 1845, in his *Theses on Feuerbach,* the Sixth Thesis had clearly stated: "But the human essence is no abstraction inhering in each particular individual. In fact, it is the totality of social relations." Even earlier in 1845, the Foreword to *The Holy Family* had offered a decidedly materialistic formulation of the same essence of human nature: "Real humanism has no more dangerous adversary in Germany than spiritualism or speculative idealism, which sets 'self-consciousness' or 'spirit' in place of the real human individual." Admittedly, the term alienation [*Entfremdung*], the negative pole of the humane [*Humanum*], recedes somewhat in the later writings of Marx, but this recession is confined only to the term and not the thing itself, oriented to the human ideal. In the later analyses of the proletarian working day and the rest of the totality of social relations as they have developed for the proletariat, the humane remains the guide and standard. Rather than list numerous available

22

examples, let us note one that is particularly late and particularly striking: "The realm of freedom actually begins only when labor, conditioned by need and external necessity, ceases; therefore, in the nature of the case, it lies beyond the sphere of particular material production" (*Capital,* III).

The "release of the richness of human nature" that will blossom on the ground of conquered necessity does not in the slightest imply the suppression of "real humanism," but, on the contrary, the establishment for the first time of its proper dignity. Humanitarianism finds a place where democracy has been made really possible, for true democracy is the first really human domicile. For Marx, the humane, even as a remote goal of the tendency of society, is completely dominant. Marxism properly pursued, effectively unburdening itself, and emancipating itself from evil neighbors, has been since its inception "humanity in action," the human countenance coming to fulfillment. It seeks, strikes out upon, and follows the one objectively real path toward this goal; hence only its future is at one and the same time inevitable and congenial.

Secularization and the Power to Set Things Upright

The humane element must be brought out into fresh and bracing air if it is to advance from mere inwardness, long enough preached in vain. Yet some now maintain (even though their opinions are of suspect origin) that this would be regressive rather than a progress. In this interpretation, whatever is set upon its feet and put into motion undergoes, so to speak, only a process of reduction from horse to mule and then to plebian pedestrian: it is sacrilegiously taken down from its sacred tabernacle and "rendered worldly." In its historical manifestation this process is also called "secularization," with less derogatory connotations. Hence the State transformed ecclesiastical into temporal lands, goods, and rights—in Germany in 1648, and more thoroughly in 1803; in France in

23

1789, and most recently in 1906. But secularization has become wholly pejorative now that the term is used in a reactionary fashion to refer to Marx—because he did so much setting things on their feet and putting them into action. It is said that Marx deflated man and his spiritual life, which were manifestly higher and more elevated before him; that the blessed life became just a happy one, endowed only with material goods; and that he sold (thus the bank clerks of the Idea) stocks which formerly had a very high quotation at a very reduced price, accessible to far too many, thus making the article so obtained worth just as little. A true connoisseur of such wares need pay no attention (so they say) to a cut-rate merchant like Marx; the expert in the wares of peace can ignore him. The true lover of man and his salvation should return to the real sources of value which he will find where the "political melody" has not yet sounded at all, or even appears to have sounded wrongly. This is a respectable way to shrug off Marx and remain sensitive to the dawn ahead and the new beginning. In this interpretation, however, the dawn is thought to have glowed in the remotest past, and the new beginning to lie behind a sacred mist instead of the so-called barren "late period" of the present. Marx himself is held to be wholly decadent, or at least an advocate of civilization in the bad sense. Just as once, from a reactionary perspective, poets were distinguished from mere writers, the latter being regarded as comparatively trivial, so the secularizing Marx has come to be regarded as a prophet of an asphalt culture. All because man and the profound implications of the humane were re-established within the possibilities of their proper stature.

This denigration of one's own age is widespread among the bourgeoisie in other ways, and not restricted to Marx. Of course, the fatigue of a declining class no longer permits much self-confidence in accordance with Spengler's description of this state. We are now in a "late period" [Spätezeit], and there is nothing else; a sterile "waking state" [Wachheit] replaces the once young "culture bearing soul" [kulturträgerische Seele]. Toynbee takes this view much farther when he represents his own "democracy and science" as secularized, and as "an almost meaningless repetition of things which the Greeks and Romans before us had already achieved, and that extraordinarily well" (*Civilization on Trial,* 1948). Yet this rejection of one's own, already historical, bourgeois values would not fulfill its social mission without a simultaneous rejection of the liberal past, as, above all, the vocation of our time with respect to the *future.* How comforting it would be if Marxism, too (indeed, especially Marxism), even on purely chronological grounds, in view of its value stance in the general autumn of culture, were in no way noteworthy, or even future sustaining. Yet how dispiriting it would be, especially for young people with a disposition or inclination toward socialism. Then Marx would not only be, as the Nazis put it, the "very depths of the nineteenth century"; even if he were and expressed the twentieth century, he would offer only the past, not the future. And the antiquarian Marx-killers do not stop here: their denigration of their own time would not be complete without idolatry of the magical moonlit nights of the past. "The revolt of the masses," "the rule of the plebs," "the noise of the mob" at the end of all the concerts of culture would not seem so wretched and pitiable but for the fact that its own music might be represented as a mere derivation from better, more spiritual, idealistic, and imaginative times. But without such a sound from the past, the process of corrective re-establishment would not be complete, and the whole business of secularization would not be destructive at the point that most concerns capitalism. In the Preface to the second edition of *Capital,* Marx first explained the process of setting upright something from the past, with special reference to the Hegelian dialectic, which was "standing on its head": "It must be turned right side up again if you would discover the rational kernel within the mystical shell." Of course, in keeping with the comparatively popular conception of Marxism's indebtedness to German classical philosophy, this process was construed not as "rescue" but equally as regression, that is, into an ostensibly unique classical tradition. Hence the once common

25

"emendations" of Marx via a Marburgian Kant or (much more weakly) a neo-Hegelian Hegel. In this way, Marxism was not yet irrationalized, but idealized, that is, it was forced back, without regard to its unique proletarian-revolutionary source, to still rationalistic though decisively non-materialistic theories.

Subsequently, however, an increasingly irrationalistic tendency developed in late bourgeoisdom, above all in Germany. Marx was now belittled by playing off quite mystical originals against their alleged imitations. The former Kantianization or Hegelianization of Marx was now accompanied by a radical attempt to destroy him by making him out to be a virtual plagiarist. The result was a quite ludicrous variety of source fetishism, tracing a line back from Marx to Joachim of Fiore or Augustine, or ultimately to primeval salvation myths. That great heretic and dreamer of future times, Joachim of Fiore, was acceptable, even though he too was only a sort of Isaiah of the thirteenth century. But Marx, because he was the crucial case, was laid hold of and unmasked as a *soi-disant* despoiler of churches—in the descrescendo of a secularization reeking of the charnel house of revolution. In this interpretation, humanitarianism was merely a trivialized version of the theme of the Son of man, proletarian solidarity was simply a vulgarized descendant of early Christian agape-communism, and the realm of freedom was simply the kingdom of the children of God—at the level of a godless pseudo-Enlightenment. In other words, the "adventures of ideas" (as Whitehead significantly terms them), whereby ideas are not worth a powder shot—although they may earn one if they cease to be spiritual. Characteristic of this line of interpretation was, for example, Löwith's source hunting for the mythological grandmother, at least a subsidiary purpose of which was to represent the grandson as someone who squanders the ancient temple treasure, in the double sense of the word. Here exploitation becomes "prehistory" or, biblically, the "original sin of this aeon," historical materialism as a whole becomes "salvation history in the language of political economy," and the "com-

26

KARL MARX AND HUMANITY: THE MATERIAL OF HOPE

munist faith a pseudomorphosis of Jewish-Christian messianism" (*Weltgeschichte und Heilsgeschehen,* 1953). With a Marx so deeply involuted, so relentlessly debunked as a plagiarist, and so magically dissolved, it is no surprise that Löwith could assert: "Compared to Marx, Hegel's philosophy is realistic." This is what results when the power to stand something the right way up, and to save the rational kernel, is interpreted exclusively as secularization—as something which is not calculated to gladden the hearts of the devotees and guides of spiritual principalities.

But a society without masters and slaves is clearly the very thing sought for so long—and in vain—under the name of humanization. It is the very thing that a class society has so long opposed or impeded—together with the substance of hope, which is only in the process of formation.

Surely a good content is not weakened if it is corrected, whereas the real plagiarists have before them only stale or flat fare, which was once better or at least fresher. The foremost members of this class of mechanical echoers are those who demand of the giants that they must have parents of stature. They might as well reject pilots as being derivative just because Elijah once rode through the air—and much farther.

But these "secularizers" are themselves epigonal, and genuinely so, for they are all adherents of a partial or completely reactionary romanticism. Mythology as a whole once seemed (to men like Creuzer and even Welcker) to be the original source of all science, and a kind of clairvoyance before the dawn of the day of mere brain power. Indeed, mythology was regarded as being the unachieved totality of knowledge from time immemorial; all subsequent endeavor which provided any knowledge (as, for example, Plato's theory of ideas) was only an echo thereof, and hence only a secularization. But Marx wrote to Ruge in 1843: "It will be shown . . . that the world has long possessed in dream form something of which it need only become conscious in order to possess it in actuality. It will then be evident that it is a question not of a great theoretical gap between past and future, but rather of realizing

27

the ideas of the past." According to the pattern of the "secularizers," such a statement would be *secularized from a romantic original,* whereas it represents an absolutely original utterance. Marx's formulation represents a *completely new* point of view in respect to the past; or, more precisely, as Marx himself says, entailing an "analysis of the mythical consciousness in the past which is unclear about itself," and of course, involving no abstract rupture with the past. *Hence a good content is actually not weakened when corrected; even more surely, it is not secularized when, having been set right way up, it is made actual.*

It is superfluous here to emphasize the completely new elements that Marx, with the proletarian-revolutionary mandate behind him, had to discover in order to be able to realize the good ideas of the past: the crucially new elements in the recognition of surplus value, in the economic-dialectical interpretation of history, in the theory-action (praxis) relationship. If the "secularizers" do not understand these matters, do not wish to do so because of their bourgeois vested interest, or cannot do so because of ignorance, this tells us something about their own reactionary attitude, but nothing about Marxism.

Least of all does this backwardness say anything about the new humanism, activism, and transformation of the world, or the adjusted forward-dreaming in Marxism, which has always remained open. Here there is no *ci-devant* myth to become cracked and thawed, but a rending of the veil, and a steady shining forth of light. In this connection, and to remain outside the Marxist process of re-establishment, let us glance at *morality.* Is morality attenuated if it is no longer practiced for the sake of an other-worldly reward? Is it not rather enhanced? And is Christianity itself made less potent (say by a Thomas Münzer) when no longer interpreted quietistically, or in the somewhat tepid other-worldly sense of "feasting on Christ's account"? On the contrary, surely Christianity becomes more genuine and an actual self-fulfillment through involvement in activity, in temporal history, in revolution, and in every other

28

"embodiment of Christ" which had appeared to the Anabaptists, and earlier to the Hussites, as mystical democracy. And let us look at the *history of science* which, among the Greeks at any rate, arose when a break with mythology was effected, even though myth was frequently, with varying emphasis, included in the elucidation of the concept. Did philosophy and science become poorer as a consequence? Surely their range of vision and knowledge was extended when Socrates sought to bring them down to earth from heaven. Or when Democritus' *ananke* by no means secularized the mythical *Moira* or goddess of fate. Or when Aristotle, with his brace of ontological concepts, *dynamis-enteleche,* and matter-form, brought to the mythical woman-man hypostases, apart from the usefulness of these concepts in demythologization, something thoroughly new, responsible, and defensible "in truth." Of course, there is a true intellectual intention within the mythical or mystical shell, something that in humanitarianism and in dialectics (already present in Chinese myth) is seeking orientation to an essential illumination that has yet to shine forth in the future; above all in the messianic lightning flashes of myth. The friend of true enlightenment will hardly withhold his delight at and gratitude for such prefigurations and their instruction. But the activity of the intellect involving the processes of amending, augmenting, and illuminating the world from the basis of the world always starts out from a scientifically achieved awareness that retains a certain given content. But this process can no longer expand and be understood in a society in which, as Edward Spranger has said, only two philosophies are left: one of desperation, which surrenders everything, and one of cobwebs, which seeks to derive ecclesiastical conclusions from medieval scholastic postulates of wisdom derived from a remote past. Only creative Marxism is appropriate to our time, for only Marxism sees it as simultaneously productive, inheriting, and fulfilling. Only in creative Marxism is humanitarianism no longer confined to human hearts or idealistic stimuli (without entailing the expenditure of a penny in the process). Only in creative Marxism may the

29

earth be said to be on the point of penetrating the world and not remaining just a mythical picture of the kind with which the "fictitious riches" of the verbal myth regurgitation of today is satisfied.

A different prospect is allowed the realization of what is correctly known, and known to be correct. It is envisioned in a tendency conceived in Marxist terms, according to the criterion of real possibility and its perspective. This is praxis: secularization indeed—but of the celestial, for it removes everything above, in which man is not apparent. Here, of course, secularization has to be understood in a really new, primarily Marxist, sense, in keeping with the theory-practice concept. Then, with proper irony, the word, made so malicious and derogatory, is redeemed in a manner which the sciolists among the detractors of Marxism could scarcely have conceived. When all the great thinkers before Marx had remained essentially satisfied to develop the world philosophically in a book, Marxist humanism appeared on the horizon to begin an actual incorporation of philosophy into the world, *suo modo.* Philosophy was set completely on its feet and enabled to stand upright, and thus it showed itself equally called to and adept in the reconstruction of the earth.

All this took place without any diminution of the great ideas of the past; the process was philosophically profound and for this very reason not poor in deeds. In Hölderlin's poem *To the German People,* the Marxist question is stated thus, after the judgment that the Germans are poor in deeds but rich in ideas: "Or will deeds like light from the clouds shine from thoughts? Will these dry books live?" A task so clearly and decisively manifest is the best possible evidence that hope conceived will be brought to birth.

Dreaming Ahead, Sobriety, Enthusiasm, and Their Unity

No dreaming may stand still, for this bodes no good. But if it becomes a dreaming ahead, then its cause appears quite

30

differently and excitingly alive. The dim and weakening features, which may be characteristic of mere yearning, disappear; and then yearning can show what it really is able to accomplish. It is the way of the world to counsel men to adjust to the world's pressures, and they have learned this lesson; only their wishes and dreams will not hearken to it. In this respect virtually all human beings are futuristic; they transcend their past life, and to the degree that they are dissatisfied, they think they deserve a better life (even though this may be pictured in a banal and egoistic way), and regard the inadequacy of their lot as a *barrier,* and not just as the way of the world.

To this extent, the most private and ignorant wishful thinking is to be preferred to any mindless goose-stepping; for wishful thinking is capable of revolutionary awareness, and can enter the chariot of history without necessarily abandoning in the process the good content of dreams. The chariot is not so cramped as bleak, miserable, or ignorant ages have pictured it or have found fitting for themselves. Social progress definitely does require, sometimes in a harsh manner, that prejudices, false consciousness, and superstition be discarded and left behind, but for this very reason it never demands that dreams toward the future be abandoned. That which is objectively possible, that to which the dream must attach itself if it is to amount to anything, also holds on to the dream in a pre-ordaining manner.

A daydream about a perfect life that is objectively mediated, and therefore can be retained, thereby overcomes its predisposition to be duped as well as any tendency to dreamlessness itself. The latter, which is associated with standing still or with a realism which only appears to be such, even in a state of resignation, is actually the ruling state of mind of many thinking though unperceptive people in a society without perspectives (and with an abundance of inaccuracy). All such people are listless or morose about the future and the view ahead, though in various ways and with different expressions of diffidence. Half a measure of Greek humility and half of positivistic caution have been dragooned in order to make an

31

anti-Marxist metaphor, so to speak, out of the fact that one cannot see around a corner, the goal of the entire effort being to remain in a state of interested dreamlessness. Yet the simple truth of the fact of not being able to see around a corner becomes nullified as soon as a mirror is used; above all, it is certainly possible to hear around a corner, and so to perceive the trend—the sort of turn that might be taken after the next bend in the road: and it is possible actively to advance this dialectical transition. Furthermore, reason has an acoustic sense of significance.

Yet dreamlessness as destiny imposes a further restriction in that the corner, and even more its non-bourgeois background (which exercises an unpleasant precursory influence), actually appears as eschatological—and accordingly employs Greek humility as a weapon against Christian forwardness. More precisely, the attack is leveled, not against Christianity as the voice of Patmos, but only against the eschatology; and remarkably this is what Marxism is here again held to be: just as though it were a super-world replete with mad frenzy and not what it so impressively is, namely, this very world, but provided with a penetrating analysis of its motivations and a sovereign anticipation of its possible good fruits.

Yet it is precisely this impressive forcefulness, in recognition of its disturbing diagnoses and prophecy, which may appear not only incisive but penetrating. This happens particularly when an abundance of inexactitude and another fullness of obviously macabre superficial brilliance hides the emptiness of one's own evening—or the fullness of another's morning, which as ever comes into being painfully.

Then dreamlessness in regard to the future may appear to be a philosophical defense; yet it is hardly truly philosophic, for it does not anticipate things to come. In this voluntary-involuntary skepticism, therefore, there is fear, not hope; and instead of an understanding of the future as the greater dimension of the present (as Leibniz said), there is only an anti-climax—with the inevitable result of separation, if not of foundering with eyes averted. Fear above all, Sartre says, is

32

the condition that abrogates man; in point of fact, the enlivening opposite is true of hope, both subjectively and—even more so—objectively. If in the building of mere castles in the air there is little concern about the expense, which results ultimately in false paths and deception, even then, in the long run, hope (with a plan and with a link with the potentially possible) is still the strongest and best thing we have. And even if hope merely overtops the horizon, whereas only knowledge of the real is able by action to move it firmly ahead, it is hope alone which enables the enkindling and comforting understanding of the world (to which it leads) to be attained as the most solid and tendentially concrete form of comprehension of the mundane. Admittedly, the comfort provided by this understanding of the world must be won laboriously. It would have been easier to build Rome in a day than Athens; and what a difficult and often painfully slow road stretches forward to the inauguration of the *regnum humanum.* "But socialist realism must have a perspective, or else it cannot be socialist"—as Lukács has said of the desired direction. Reason cannot blossom without hope, and hope cannot speak without reason: both must operate in a Marxist unity; no other science has a future, no other future has science.

An upright carriage distinguishes us from the beasts; but we are still without it. As yet it is present only as a wish, as the desire for a life without exploitation and overlords. The daydream, as enduring as it is necessary, has hovered over what has hitherto taken place, and previous failures, and has looked ahead. And occasional seekers of the upright posture have marched on before, in keeping with Ludwig Börne's admonition: "Before an age breaks camp and moves forward, it always sends ahead able and reliable men as scouts for the next site. If these messengers are permitted to go their way, and they are followed and kept in sight, the new way of the epoch is soon recognized. But if the scouts are called agitators, seducers, and enthusiasts, and are forcibly restrained, there will be no such vision. Then time and all its complete baggage moves ahead, and finding nothing arranged and ordered, settles down where it pleases, taking and destroying more than it uses or wants."

This situation has certainly changed since Marx, especially where Marxism has become a power—and the future was billetted. Moreover, the daydream of the *regnum humanum* is no longer set in the air or the heavens, or merely in works of art, where the paths to it are taken only as roads of escape, and the sort of resignation goes out to them for which beauty blossoms only in song. Opportunity is now given to a gold other than Mammon to precipitate itself out of the traditional utopian-ideology mess. Yet anticipation must blossom and still has its own function, particularly when it occurs in *sobriety,* rather than in fog and cloud.

Enthusiasm assists sobriety in order to prevent a shortening of the perspective in some abstract-immediate fashion, and to keep it on the plane of concrete possibility. Enthusiasm is imagination in action, and here the acid of sobriety must become the most precious rather than the most common and cheap ingredient.

Nothing is more distant from true Marxist sobriety than common sense, which is not so healthy and not so human, but is more likely to be replete with petit bourgeois prejudices. On the other hand, nothing is closer to genuine sobriety than the quality of *bon sens,* as found in Marxist enthusiasm. Common sense, typically undialectical, asserts that men will always be men, and (if its possessor has spent his life in Central Africa) that it is absurd to think that water could occur in solid form. Similarly, common sense has maintained that China could never become a republic. On the other hand, *bon sens,* the sign of truly healthy sobriety, does not exclude any perspective except one that could lead to a situation without good fortune. This is especially characteristic of Marxism as the billeting officer of the future. It overcomes the rigid antithesis of sobriety versus enthusiasm by bringing them both to a new state, and enabling both to work together for precise anticipation and concrete utopia. It is not the function of sobriety merely to remove fantasy; and it is not the function of

34

enthusiasm, precisely as imagination in action, to operate exclusively with absolutes, as though revolutionary romanticism coincided with quixotism. To set the hour hand of a clock one must turn the minute hand; similarly but conversely, the whole of a great vessel embarked on a long journey must be clearly apparent in all the minutiae of revolutionary activity. It is unwise, and alien to Marxism, to underreach reality with sobriety alone or conversely to overreach it with nothing but enthusiasm for it. The reality, especially that of the historical trend, is encountered only through the permanent interplay of both aspects united in a responsibly educated perspective. Hence, on the fourth anniversary of the October revolution, Lenin wrote: "Not on the foundation of enthusiasm pure and simple but with the support of the enthusiasm born of the great revolution, on the basis of personal interest, personal involvement, and the principle of profitability, you must first of all strive to build the sound roads which, in a petit bourgeois country, will lead to socialism via state capitalism. Otherwise you will never achieve communism, otherwise you will never lead myriads of people to communism." Closely bound up with this cool realism, however, is the objectively committed factor which Lenin referred to in his essay on "'Left-Wing' Communism," as appropriate to the dynamic *élan* in (and not to the slowing down of) reality: "History generally, and the history of revolutions in particular, is always richer in content, more varied, more many-sided, more lively, and 'subtle' than the best parties and the most class-conscious vanguards of the most advanced classes imagine. This is understandable, because the best vanguards express the class-consciousness, the will, the passion, the fantasy of tens of thousands, while the revolution is made, at the moment of its climax and of the exertion of all human capabilities, by the class-consciousness, the will, the passion, the imagination of tens of millions."

And the paradigm for the cold shower needed for the sake of this warm current (this latter needing the cold shower of analysis precisely in order to demonstrate its several stages) is obviously to be found in Marx himself, in his empirical

35

ON KARL MARX

prophecy: "Justice can never be higher than the economic structure of society and the cultural development conditioned by that structure. In a higher phase of communist society, when the enslaving subordination of the individual to the division of labor, and with it the antithesis between physical and intellectual labor, has disappeared; when labor has become not only a means of life but life's prime need, when the forces of production have grown with the all-around development of the individual, and all the springs of cooperative wealth flow more abundantly: only then will the narrow horizon of bourgeois justice be completely transcended, and society write on its banners: 'From each according to his abilities, to each according to his needs'" *(A Critique of the Gotha Program).*

Only with such an *analysis* (and even, at times, an analysis *ad pessimum,* in view of a particularly hazardous channel), and only with such a *perspective* does that comforting understanding of the world known as Marxism result, which is not contemplation but a directive for action. The incompatibility of the productive forces (which have long since become social) and their private capitalist form of appropriation is a basic persistent contradiction in a developed capitalist society that can be only superficially hidden by hectic economic fluctuations between crises, and by quack theories. Only Marxism, however, both detects and liberates, providing both the theoretical and the practical solution for this so long-standing contradiction. Furthermore, only Marxism has produced the theory and practice of a better world, not in order to abrogate the present one, as in most of the abstract social utopias, but in order to transform this world economically and dialectically. Marxism never renounces its heritage, and least of all the primal intention: the Golden Age. In all its *analyses* Marxism plays the part of a sober detective, yet takes the legend seriously, and reacts pragmatically to the *dream of the Golden Age.* The primary concern has been the debit and credit of real hope. Until now the conditions have not made it possible to enter actively into near-perfect perspectives, and certainly not into the relationships of the perfect society, for it does not actually exist as yet, and in the alienation experienced has been kept especially distant.

The relationship of need to the warmth and enthusiasm in most of the wishful daydreams produced in the past was (beyond contemplation) resignation, or (close to it in this connection) religion. But if the real essence of the contents of hope enters adequately into existence, winning firm ground and stability, then the point of entry, equipped conjointly with *prosaic* and *symbolic value,* is the classless society—*usque ad finem.*

Certainty, Unfinished World, Home

> There came to him here an image of man's whole life upon the earth. It seemed to him that all man's life was like a tiny spurt of flame that blazed out briefly in an illimitable and terrifying darkness, and that all man's grandeur, tragic dignity, his heroic glory, came from the brevity and smallness of this flame. He knew his life was little and would be extinguished, and that only darkness was immense and everlasting. And he knew that he would die with defiance on his lips, and that the shout of his denial would ring with the last pulsing of his heart into the maw of all-engulfing night.
>
> THOMAS WOLFE, *You Can't Go Home Again*

> The wish builds and produces something actual. We alone are the gardeners of the most mysterious tree that may grow. The drive to become adequate to oneself draws the soul in. It is the resolution of thought for the perfect crystallization of renewed reality, and of the mind dissolving and yet resolving all creatively. It is strong as a magnet pointing into our future and that of the world, as the future ever

37

gazes after us and alone offers, with equal indeci-
siveness, to laggard choice, evil as well as good. It
revolves about us and does not know where it is
going; but we ourselves are still lever and motor;
the outer and revealed life are held in check. But
finally the new thought does break out into the
fullness of adventure, into the open, unfinished,
noisy world, so that, in its own strength, fortified
with our suffering, and with our daring premonition,
with the tremendous force of our human voice, it
may pronounce God's name and not rest until our
innermost shadows have surrendered, and that
empty, seething night is filled around about which
all things, men, and works are still built.

ERNST BLOCH, *Spirit of Utopia,* 1918

Three categories of the dialectical process are . . .
central: Front, *Novum,* and Matter. All three pre-
suppose the most worthy human capacity for comprehension and participation: namely, hope. *Front*
is the foremost segment of time, where what is next
is determined. *Novum* is the real possibility of the
not-yet-known, not-yet-wrought-into-being, with
the accent of the good *novum* (the realm of freedom), when the trend toward it has been activated.
Matter is not just mechanical mass, but—in accordance with the implicit meaning of the Aristotelian definition of matter—both that which has being
in accordance with possibility, and hence that
which in a particular case conditionally determines
the capacity of something to become historically
manifest, and that-which-exists-in-possibility, and
hence the real possibility substrate of the dialectical
process. Precisely as being in movement, matter is
being that is not yet manifest; it is the ground and
substance in which our future—its own future

too—is carried out. Hence there are many problems for contemporary philosophy; although they are overdue for consideration by the West today, they are, paradoxically, not ripe enough.

Therefore, the old tag *ex oriente lux,* favored by geographers and Christians alike, is allowed a new truth: light comes from the orient-point of modern man. German philosophy from Hegel to Marx first articulated this truth, and must continue to recognize its responsibility in this regard.

ERNST BLOCH, *Philosophy Today,* 1950

Rectified wishing, too, does not give up or renounce. It does not vanish, no matter how difficult and costly it turns out to be. It does not cling fast to the given, but finds it fitting, while it can glimpse what is extant and visible, not to believe in it entirely. On the other hand, the subjective hope with which people hope is sure of itself and secure, even when that which it designates, namely, the objective hope in the substance of which hope is placed, can at best be only probable. The subjective hope is *spes qua speratur,* while the objective is *spes quae speratur.* The first, the hoping hope, is also really believed in and so has conviction *suo modo;* whereas if the second, the hope that is hoped, already had full conviction for itself, it would really not be hope. This means that the matter designated in the hope that is hoped, so unbending yet actively enkindling until the last—the *objective substance* of hope in the world itself—is as yet by no means guaranteed to be secure and certain of itself. Otherwise, the conviction of hoping hope would be simply trivial rather than brave and, as so frequently happens, quite paradoxical. Authentic hope as such—that is, when mediated by an historical trend—stands least of all in an empty space, from which nothing will approach it, and in which any venture is indeterminate. Precisely because genuine hope within the world proceeds by way of the world and works through the mediation of the world's objective process, it is engaged in a venture together with this process, and they stand in the *front line* together.

Only when the duly expected and attainable goal of socialist humanization is not obscured by inadequacy and harshly delayed by deviations can the objectively valid laws of dialectical development and their ultimate possibility act as effective guides and be appropriately nurtured. In and by itself, hoping hope may be altogether decisive, yet the outcome itself still has to be determined, in open history as the field of objectively real decision. This is the category of hazard or of objective non-warrantability—even of mediated hope, or *docta spes*. As yet there is no settled absence of problems as with a fixed result. Such security does not yet exist in the dark sense whereby decision making, *novum,* and objective possibility would be extinguished, and not every lost battle could be more proficiently fought another time.

Nor is there yet any lack of problems in the supremely luminous sense of an existence without alienation, and of unambiguously matured and naturalized value. Consequently, optimism is justified only as militant, never as confirmed. In the latter form its effect, so far as the misery of the world is concerned, is not only evil but senseless. And really perfect decisiveness exists just as little in any fashion or place in a hypostatized other world, as though the *ens perfectissimum* of the beyond were some superior *ens realissimum* enthroned. This kind of perfected "fact" of a higher order, as posited not only by theistic religions but by metaphysical idealisms, represents no more than a pure hypostasis.

It is even worse, even more false, that all previous philosophies, to the extent that they have envisaged such remote celestial areas, have dealt with their god, substance, or absolute, as though it were some unequalled fixed point of orientation, a *fixum,* a *definitum,* and even an incomparable *realissimum,* and as though all process were simply pedagogic guidance toward such a fixed point of orientation or away from it.

40

Certainly human life is entirely and primarily a process of transcending, a stepping beyond the given; but with equal certainty, this sort of transcending, being concretely utopian, involves no transcendence, which would itself be a finished, phantom given. As surely as the conscience of concrete utopia does not cling positivistically to the fact of *direct visibility,* even more surely it does not ascend in a vaporous mist of mere fact hypostases of purely *mythological invisibility.*

Instead, philosophy authenticates itself as expedition with and in the widely ramified and unfinished process, as the courage required for that non-warrantability *which sets hope squarely at the front.* Philosophy does not prove itself by interpreting an unfinished state as fate, nor merely by an infinite process of drawing near a goal, as (symbolically) in Tantalus and (morally) in Kant. For the unfinished world can be brought to an end, and the process pending in it can be brought to a result; and the incognito of the main concern that is actually concealed even to itself can be illuminated. But not by premature hypostases or fixed determinations of essence, which only block the way. The real nature or the essence is not something already found in a finished form, like water, air, or fire, or even an invisible universal idea, or whatever figure may be used to absolutize or hypostatize these real quanta. The real or the essence is that *which does not yet exist, which is in quest of itself in the core of things, and which is awaiting its genesis in the trend latency of the process.* It is in itself the just-founded, objectively real hope. Moreover, its name ultimately has points of contact with "being-in-possibility" in the Aristotelian sense, and indeed, in a sense that goes far beyond him, with that which is patently most established, namely, matter. All its bearing, conditioning, and becoming would be senseless were everything that might and could emerge from it already extant. Of course, the Not-Yet must not be thought of as though there already existed, say in the atom or in the subatomic "differentials" of matter, everything that would later emerge, already present and encapsulated in miniscule form as inherent "disposition." Such a backward conception of the Not-Yet would

41

really undercut or misconstrue the dialectical leap into the new.

And of course, in the dialectical trend latency of the material process, which is open to the new, there is no *pre-ordained* and therefore no settled end of the traditional teleological kind, let alone one mythologically deduced from above.

Yet the genuine problem of teleology is not discredited along with this old teleology, reminiscent of "providence": the genuine categories of end, then purpose, then meaning, are not evaded or dogmatically dismissed from the world. All the less since a tendency always implies orientation to a goal, and any progress without such a reference to a given end can neither be measured nor have any objective reality. All the less since a world without efficient planning with and for it, without operational goals, purposes, and meanings within it, could in no sense be a Marxist one. Therefore, the *truth* of teleology nowhere consists of ends present in a finished form, but rather of goals which first receive form in the active process, rising therein ever anew, and gaining power for themselves. The nerve of the genuine historical concept is the *novum;* and the nerve of the authentically philosophical concept is the better *novum.* Moreover, the utopian tenor in so many, if not most, doctrines of essence is hidden only because the purposive truth of all things was represented as already existing absolutely, and therefore as completely exhibited. This truth, as the appropriateness of things to itself, its exhaustive and fundamental essence, thereupon passes as complete in itself, clear, brought forth, and still veiled only for man's feeble powers of comprehension. From the trial examples, which, so to speak, represent the individual metaphysical titles of the essence, there arises the *exemplum* itself; from the experiments concerning the real-unique, there results an almost fixed and, at that, highly contemplative ontology. The observational nature of most pre-Marxist philosophers thus consummates an extreme degree of present availability—even though it is still, with much polyphonic light, only in the condition of predictability. With such ontic hypostatization the method becomes

42

purely a way of consummation; the result becomes a palace, somehow complete at the end of the way; and the metaphysics of *Hen Kai Pan* becomes a finished palace inscription. The net result is not only that matter is unknown, but even where it is known, its most important truth is unknown, namely, that of being matter with a forward trend.

But now not only art but philosophy—and especially the latter—has consciously to bear the responsibility of prefiguration, and the prefiguration at that of an objectively real appearance, of the *world of process, of the real world of hope itself*. Furthermore, the latter remains uniquely based in matter—in something that is certainly mobile in a polymorphic and not stereotyped manner; in that-which-is-in-accordance-with-possibility, and as such has a duly determinative effect, and in that-which-is-in-possibility, and as such has a substantively opening effect. To perceive this genesis is the function of philosophy. Its new shape is the dialectically aimed, systematically open, vista into matter as it takes tendential form.

The morrow lives in today, and is constantly inquired after. The countenances that turned in the utopian direction have been different at different times, even as the details of what they believed they saw there in each particular case. Yet the *direction* has everywhere been related, and actually, in regard to its still concealed goal, the same. Indeed, it appears to be the only constant in history. Happiness, freedom, non-alienation, the golden age, the land flowing with milk and honey, the eternal feminine, the trumpet call in *Fidelio,* and the Christ pattern of the resurrection day afterwards—there are so many and diverse witnesses and pictures, yet all have but one focus, which speaks to us eloquently, notwithstanding its silence. The orientation to this evident focus (evident not just logically but materially) must be invariant. This is recognizable wherever hope opens up its account and endeavors to read therein. There is never any doubt that an unilluminated, undirected hope easily leads men astray, for the true horizon does not reach beyond the *knowledge of realities.* But this very knowledge, when Marxist and not mechanistic, shows *reality itself as*

43

a horizon reality, and informed hope as congruous with this reality.

The goal in its entirety is and still remains concealed, and so the account of willing and hoping is still untallied; within the functioning of the process of existence, light, of its quiddity, of its essence, of its intended basic content, has not yet shone forth. Yet the *nunc stans* of the dynamic moment, of the effort filled with its content, stands forth and ahead in a utopianly clear fashion. As the restless Abelard put it: *"Terminus est illa civitas ubi non praevenit rem desiderium nec desiderio minus est praemium."* "The goal is that community where the yearning for the thing does not completely anticipate it, and where the fulfillment is not less than the yearning."

This is being as hope, *quid pro quo,* namely, a something and essence such that the intention contained therein may be preserved and transcended because fulfilled. Yet the very human capacity for such an absolute goal-concept is the terrible element in an existence where the best remains only a fragment, and where every end again and again becomes only a means to serve the as yet completely invisible, final, and ultimate goal, which is as yet unavailable even in and for itself.

Marx indicates that his ultimate intention is "the development of the wealth of human nature." This *human* wealth, like that of *nature* as a whole, lies exclusively in the trend latency in which the world finds itself *vis-à-vis de tout.* In this view, therefore, it follows that man everywhere is still living in prehistory, and that all things are still in the stage prior to the just and true creation of the world. *The true genesis is not at the beginning, but at the end,* and it starts to begin only when society and existence become radical: that is, comprehend their own roots. But the root of history is the working, creating man, who rebuilds and transforms the given circumstances of the world. Once man has comprehended himself and has established his own domain in real democracy, without depersonalization and alienation, something arises in the world which all men have glimpsed in childhood: a place and a state in which no one has yet been. And the name of this something is home or homeland.

MAN AND CITIZEN IN MARX

It read differently before the meal—how often this statement
holds true. When the bourgeoisie had not come to power, it
was (or appeared to be) more humane than any previous class.
It stood for the free man, the children of the fatherland, and
universal humanity. There was a cue for the free man, the
national disposition could become nationalistic, the human
principle could become ever more universal. But what seemed
so pure in inception, and only later abandoned and indeed
reversed this orientation, once implemented, continued to
shine thus later.

Not everything read differently before the meal—as in the
present case. The image of the heritage striven for—the
citoyen—replete with illusions and indeed with even greater
anticipations, was exploited by the same economic and social
trend that later brought forth the emancipated bourgeois. And
the essence of the bourgeois, only vastly different and progressive in the wrong sense, to wit, the mere freedom of acquisition, necessarily developed together with the image of the
citizen—at least in its main aspects.

Indeed, even in 1791, when human rights were still piously
affirmed, in those vernal fantasies which never came to

46

fruition, there was already something of the bourgeois spirit which certainly did flourish later on. At that time it was the bourgeois, the egotistic dynamics of individual production, but not as yet the *citizen* with actual freedom, equality, and fraternity, that constituted the economic program of the day. Private property was one of the essential components of the four bourgeois human rights of 1791; *"propriété"* dominates the *"sûreté,"* the *"résistance."* Above all, private property determines the content of freedom, according to the constitution of 1793, Art. 16: "The right of property devolves to every citizen; he may at will [*à son gré*] enjoy his fortune, his income, and the fruits of his toil and diligent effort, and dispose of them."

This decline in the stature of the citizen corresponded to the interests of capitalism, even before Thermidor, insofar as the nation had not yet surrendered the ground in which the flowers of true freedom bloom. Or, as Marx says, insofar as the people did not possess the idea of their own real interest when they accepted the idea of the French Revolution. In this way, Marx carefully distinguished the egotistic contents of the *droits de l'homme* of that time from the then political, still abstract and idealistic, ideal-construct of the *citoyen*. The local impetus behind the precision of this differentiation was the arrogant nonsense of Bruno and Edgar Bauer, who had declared that the pure idea of the French Revolution had been corrupted by the "uncritical masses." Instead, Marx and Engels pointed to the complete success of this revolution as the emancipation of the bourgeois, and the profit system then required by the economy—a reference which could not be made without sharp criticism of the ideology of human rights itself.

Yet beyond this particular case, every reception of the socialist heritage must be critical, and none must have a wax figure crowned with laurel. To begin with, bourgeois freedoms are always more bourgeois than they are freedoms. The assessment of the Rights of Man in regard to their ideological content is perfectly understandable; and the first results of such a scrutiny were caution, partial negation, and restriction.

47

Thus Marx declares in *On the Jewish Question* (1844): "The so-called Rights of Man, the *droits de l'homme,* in contrast to the *droits du citoyen,* are nothing more than the rights of the member of civil society, that is, of egotistic man, separated from his fellow men and from the community . . . Hence man is not liberated from religion, but merely obtains religious freedom. He is not liberated from property, but only obtains the freedom of property. He is not emancipated from the egotism of commerce, but obtains freedom for commerce" (MEGA, I, 1, p. 593). Subsequently, in *The Holy Family* (1845), he wrote: "Even the slavery of civil society appears to be the greatest freedom, because the apparently accomplished independence of the individual fosters the illusion of the limitless motility of the alienated elements of his life (such as property, industry, and religion, which have been freed of general restrictions and are no longer bound by other people) as personal freedom. In truth, however, this limitless motility is to be interpreted as the individual's complete enslavement and dehumanization . . . What a colossal deception, to have to recognize and sanction under the aegis of human rights, the modern bourgeois society, the society of industry and of general competition, of private interest, freely pursuing their goals; of anarchy, of alienated natural and spiritual individuality—and at the same time, within this society, to annul the expressions of life . . . in particular individuals, while simultaneously intending to fashion the political head of this society to a classical pattern" (MEGA, I, 3, pp. 291 ff.). These are the same self-deceptions which Marx later, at the very beginning of *The Eighteenth Brumaire* (1852), termed "a conjuring up of the dead of world history."

From this critique there emerged a significant positive element, relating not to human rights in general, but to the "rights of the *citoyen.*" Marx refers at the beginning of the same work to the self-deceptions of Robespierre, and of Cromwell before him, as "those needed by them in order to conceal from themselves the bourgeois limitations of the content of their struggles, and to maintain their passion at the high level of great historical tragedy." It was necessary, therefore, "to glorify the new struggles . . . to magnify in imagination the given task . . . to find anew the spirit of revolution." Note: "the *spirit of revolution.*" It was to this that the "rights of the *citoyen*" held fast. And this spirit becomes realized, as Marx finally observes—after all this criticism—in his *On the Jewish Question,* "only when the real, individual man takes into himself again the abstract citizen of the state . . . only when man recognizes and organizes his *forces propres*—his own powers—as *social* powers, and so no longer separates social power from himself, in the form of political power" (MEGA, I, 1, p. 599).

The abstract citizen of the state, wrenched away from the "secular man" albeit contained in him, the "true man" thus brought into relief, this is the *citoyen;* yet he is this also as the "political power," as the bearer of socialized freedom. In this view, the fellow man no longer represents, as in the egotism of the *droits de l'homme,* a barrier to freedom, but rather its fulfillment. Nonetheless, the image of the *citoyen,* when still in the bourgeois womb, so to speak, suffered an injury which has exercised its effects subsequently, because it was not recognized initially. But the whole image of the *citoyen,* notwithstanding its diverse sources, and even its pernicious stewards, continued—even as a slogan—to exert an effective critical force against its contrary, as it developed; indeed, it always contained within itself, as Hölderlin showed, renewed self-purification.

From this point on, Marx permitted a much warmer light to fall even on the rights of man. With unsurpassed precision, he demonstrated the bourgeois class content in them, yet at the same time their futuristic outlook, which at that time still had no basis. He discovered private property as dominant among the other human rights, and the reason why the others appeared all the more disjointed. When Marx denounces private property as the bourgeois barrier to human rights, he does not reject freedom, the resistance of the people to oppression, and security, as other rights. But he concentrated on the forward

49

effect of Right, which no private property can impede or ultimately destroy. Marx criticized private property by the standard of the very radiance and humanity of the human right to freedom. Freedom is the viewpoint from which his conclusions follow: not freedom of property but freedom from property; not freedom of industry but from the egotism of industry; not emancipation of the egotistic individual from merely feudal society but the emancipation of all men from every type of class society. In so thorough a fashion, then, *liberté* rather than *propriété* ultimately became dominant among the rights of man, and an actual and effective autonomous goal opposed to fascism, and even to dictatorship. Subsequently, the struggle for rights concentrated more on freedom of assembly, freedom of organization, freedom of the press, and the rights of workers to resist exploitation and oppression.

In the *program* of socialism, however, where the exploitation and oppression of the workers have disappeared, the struggle for rights has gone forward as the quest for the rights of uncompromising objective criticism, followed by pragmatic intervention, in the interests of the goal of socialist construction, within the framework of solidarity. Hence, within the socialist movement solidarity signifies that the "human" in "human rights" shall no longer represent the egotistic but the socialist individual, who, in accordance with Marx's prophecy, has transformed his own powers into socio-political power. The result would be that the *citoyen* would be pulled back out of the abstract-moralistic transcendental world which he inhabited in the ideology of the French Revolution, into the mundane world appropriate to socialized humanity.

Everywhere, however, it would be the common banner of human rights which would raise up workers in capitalistic lands in their right to resist, and which would lead the way for them in their constructive work in socialist lands through the building of socialism and the right of criticism—and indeed the obligation to do so. Otherwise, authoritarian socialism would prevail—*contradictio in adjecto*—whereas the International fought for the human right of organized maturity.

And something further shone on the old banner, formerly derided by the bourgeoisie. This was nothing less than the passion to march forward and the wise faith to serve it. Freedom leads the people: this title of a painting by Delacroix unmistakably indicated a path leading forward. It depicts a freedom which, in common progressive action, tears itself loose from the superannuated and reaches out to new shores, with the night behind it and the day ahead. The reference to "superannuated" is primarily to the relationships of production which have become shackles. That is, the new shores, as of 1791, lay at first in the realm of the emancipated egotistic individual, of free competition, the open market—in short, of the modes of production and exchange that were expanding under capitalism. For this purpose, the bourgeoisie, one of the least heroic of classes, desperately needed heroic illusion in the classical mode. Yet in the illusions contained in the Jacobin faith (those which purported to be able to liberate all the oppressed) there was operative something that was no mere borrowing from antiquity. This was an anticipation, with an aura of progress: anticipation of an immensely improved type of *polis;* and this first gave the enterprise that moral radiance which the emancipation of the third estate (and none other) lacked. It was this human right which prompted Beethoven to place a bust of Brutus in his room, which produced the music of *Fidelio,* and the Ninth Symphony for the rescue and the arrival of joy. In the novelty of the contemporary struggle for freedom there lived the ultimate of total liberation. All this Marx was alluding to when he spoke of the "spirit of revolution" which it is necessary to find anew through magnification and imagination, as against the limited "civil content."

Moreover, no matter how much previous revolutions differed in terms of their social mandate, and no matter how specifically the proletarian-socialist revolution, involving the total elimination of class society, differs from every earlier

51

one, they are all pervaded by a unifying typical and cohesive trend. This tendency relates all and every one of its *reminiscences* to the leap into the domain of freedom. The Jacobin movement manifested at least premonitions of this leap: to such a degree that the French Revolution consistently introduced socialist-humanist concepts of progress that far transcended the maturing emancipation of the entrepreneurs and their class.

The same Marx who so penetratingly analyzed the capitalist factor in the rights of man, proclaimed in *The Holy Family* what was still implicit in the Jacobins and their followers: "Secure against this opposition, the French Revolution generated ideas which led beyond those of the whole former condition of the world. The revolutionary movement which began in 1789 in the *Cercle Social,* featured in mid-course Leclerc and Roux as its chief representatives, and finally succumbed momentarily with Babeuf's conspiracy, had advanced the communistic idea, which Babeuf's friend Buonarotti reintroduced into France after the revolution of 1830. This idea, consistently developed, is the idea of the new condition of the world . . . Just as Cartesian materialism runs into natural science proper, so the other direction of French materialism culminates directly in socialism and communism" (MEGA, I, 3, pp. 294 ff.).

Thus even in the old tricolor there was a strong red gleam, announced by the fourth estate—the red of irreducible progress. This was directed against the emasculation of the time, against the alliance with the "primitive forces of life" as seen through the nobility and the church, and against a nihilism of goals in which the *Ça ira* of the French Revolution completely fades away. As against this, Marx criticized the *Ça ira* of the natural-rights slogans then current, partly for its abstraction and partly for its immobility, only in order to transcend it definitively by a further process, the socialist one. Man— *l'homme*—was static as "egotistic man," sundered from other men and the community; the *citoyen* as a mere borrowed, idealized image in a neo-classical *polis,* or as an "allegorical moral person," instead of as the bearer of social freedom, was abstract and immobile. The progress which has survived is precisely the political-civic factor: freedom, equality, and fraternity had to enter into the *"forces propres"* of living men. Indeed, only then, as Marx said, "is human emancipation accomplished." Then one's fellow man will no longer exist, as in the egotism of the *droits de l'homme,* as a barrier to freedom, but man and his fellows will live together in a community of freedom.

CHANGING THE WORLD: MARX'S *THESES ON FEUERBACH*

The Theses

1.

The main defect of all previous materialism (including that of Feuerbach) is that things, reality, the sensible world, are conceived only in the form of *objects,* or of *observation,* but not as *sensuous human activity, praxis,* not subjectively. Hence, in contradistinction to materialism, the *active* aspect of reality was developed abstractly by idealism, which, of course, does not recognize real sensuous activity as such. Feuerbach wants sensuous objects, really distinguished from objects of thought, but he does not understand human activity itself as *objective* activity. Hence, in *The Essence of Christianity,* he regards the theoretical attitude as the only genuinely human one, whereas practical activity is apprehended and fixed only in its dirty-Judaical manifestation. Consequently, he does not grasp the significance of "revolutionary," "practical-critical," activity.

54

2.

The question of whether human thinking can arrive at objective truth is not a theoretical but a practical question. Man has to prove the truth, that is, the reality and power, the "this-sidedness" of his thinking, in practice. The dispute over the reality or non-reality of thinking which is isolated from practice is a purely *scholastic* exercise.

3.

The materialist doctrine concerning the changing of circumstances and education forgets that circumstances are changed by men and that the educator has himself to be educated. Consequently, this doctrine is bound to divide society into two parts, one of which is superior to society. The coincidence of the changing of circumstances and of human activity or self-transformation can be grasped and rationally understood only as *revolutionary practice.*

4.

Feuerbach starts from the fact of religious self-alienation, the duplication of the world into a religious and a secular one. His work consists in resolving the religious world into its secular basis. But the fact that the secular basis separates itself from itself and establishes an independent realm for itself in the clouds can be explained only by the self-cleavage and self-contradictions of this secular basis. Therefore, the latter must be understood in its contradictions and revolutionized in practice. Thus, for example, once the earthly family is discovered to be the secret of the holy family, the former must itself be destroyed both in theory and in practice.

55

5.

Feuerbach is not satisfied with *abstract thought,* and desires *empirical observation.* He does not, however, conceive sensuousness as *practical* human sensuous activity.

6.

Feuerbach resolves the essence of religion into the essence of *man.* But the essence of man is no abstraction inherent in each particular individual. In its reality the essence of man is the totality of social relations. As Feuerbach does not enter upon criticism of this real essence, he is therefore obliged:

a) to abstract from the historical process, to fix the religious sentiment as something by itself, and to postulate an abstract-*isolated*-human individual;

b) consequently, to conceive the essence of man only as a "genus," as an inner, mute general quality which unites the many individuals in a purely *natural* way.

7.

Hence Feuerbach does not see that the "religious sentiment" is itself a social product, and that the abstract individual he analyzes belongs to a particular form of society.

8.

All social life is essentially *practical.* All the mysteries which lead theory to mysticism find their rational solution in human practice and in the comprehension of this practice.

9.

The highest point attained by *contemplative* materialism—materialism, that is, which does not conceive sensuousness as practical activity—is the contemplation of particular individuals and of civil society.

10.

The standpoint of the older type of materialism is civil society; the standpoint of the new materialism is human society or socialized humanity.

11.

The philosophers have only *interpreted* the world in different ways; the point is to *change* it.

Seeking the Essential

By virtue of an early flair for the essential, the nineteen-year-old Marx, as his letter to his father shows, was able to formulate sharply conceived basic propositions. This type of reasoning aims, from the very outset, at the core of the things, never permitting itself to deviate into the useless, at once ejecting the useless wherever it is recognized.

This ability to grasp the essential, regardless of the breadth of the view and the thoroughness of the analysis, always retains a striking and pointed form. That which is comprehended, which is enabled to be comprehended in such a fashion, provides pointers along the way. With them, and by means of them, the way ahead becomes clearer, so that even eventual detours serve it. Of course, such signposts are often more easily referred to than their consequences are predictable. Significant brevity is cohesive, for which reason its word is least of all expeditiously ready.

The Time of Composition

Hence the mind must constantly prove itself anew against propositions of this type. This is done with exceptional originality in the extremely compact signpost statements of the almost telegraphically compressed *Theses on Feuerbach*. Marx wrote them in Brussels during April 1845, most probably in the course of preliminary work for *The German Ideology*. They were not published by Engels until 1888, as an appendix to his *Ludwig Feuerbach and the End of Classical German Philosophy*. Engels edited the text lightly for style, since Marx had left some points practically in note form; but of course Engels made not the slightest change in the content. Concerning the *Theses*, Engels wrote in the Preface to his *Ludwig Feuerbach:* "These are notes to be elaborated later, written down in haste, and certainly not ready for the printer, yet invaluable as the first document in which the brilliant germ of the new world view is deposited."

Feuerbach had called for a return from pure thought to sensuous perception, from spirit to man, with nature as his base. As is well known, this renunciation of Hegel, at once both "humanistic" and "naturalistic" (with man as the fundamental idea, and nature instead of mind as the base [*Prius*]), exercised a powerful influence upon the young Marx. Feuerbach's *The Essence of Christianity* (1841), followed by his *Preliminary Theses toward the Reform of Philosophy* (1842), and then by his *Principles of the Philosophy of the Future* (1843), were the more liberating in their effect, seeing that even the left-Hegelian school did not tear itself away from Hegel, and indeed did not progress beyond a merely intra-Hegelian criticism of the master of idealism. Looking back as much as fifty years later, Engels observed in his *Ludwig Feuerbach:* "The enthusiasm was general. For a moment we were all Feuerbachians. How enthusiastically Marx greeted the new view, and how, despite all critical reservations, he was influenced by it anyone can read in *The Holy Family*. The German youth of that period believed that finally they were

58

seeing earth instead of heaven, in a human, this-worldly perspective."

Nevertheless, Marx fairly soon dissociated himself from this all too vague this-worldly humanism. His activity on the *Rheinische Zeitung* had brought him into much closer contact with political and economic questions than was the case with the left-Hegelians or even the Feuerbachians. This contact led Marx to develop his criticism from one religion, to which Feuerbach confined himself, into a criticism of the State and even of social organization, which determined the form of the State, as was recognized in *A Critique of Hegel's Philosophy of the State* (1841-1843). In Hegel's distinction between civil society and the State, as sharpened by Marx, there was already more economic awareness than in the imitators of Hegel, including the Feuerbachians. The separation from Feuerbach occurred respectfully and at first only as a correction or supplementation, yet the completely different viewpoint, namely, the social, is clear from the start. In a letter to Ruge of March 13, 1843, Marx observed: "Feuerbach's aphorisms appear to me to be incorrect only when he directs too much attention to nature and too little to politics. This is, however, the only alliance whereby the philosophy of today may become a truth" (MEGA, I, 1/2, p. 308).

The *Economic and Philosophic Manuscripts of 1844* still contain a significant celebration of Feuerbach, admittedly as a contrast to the cerebral fantasies of Bruno Bauer. Among Feuerbach's achievements Marx praises above all "the establishment of authentic materialism and real science by making the relation 'of man to man' the fundamental principle of this theory" (MEGA, I, 3, p. 152). Yet the *Economic and Philosophic Manuscripts* have gone further beyond Feuerbach than they would seem to indicate. Here the relation "of man to man" does not remain, as in Feuerbach, a mere abstract anthropological concept. The criticism of human self-alienation (carried over from religion to the State) already penetrates to the economic core of the alienation process. This occurs not least in the magnificent sections dealing with

59

Hegel's *Phenomenology*, in which the historically decisive role of labor is recognized, and in which Hegel's work is interpreted in this regard.

At the same time, the *Economic and Philosophic Manuscripts* criticize this work because it conceives of human labor as only mental, not material. The breakthrough to political economy, that is, away from Feuerbach's generalized man, takes place in the first work undertaken in collaboration with Engels, namely, *The Holy Family.* In the *Economic and Philosophic Manuscripts* one already finds: "Workers are themselves capital and a commodity" (MEGA, I, 3, p. 103). All that remains here of the Feuerbachian humanism [*Menschsein*] is its negation in capitalism. *The Holy Family* expresses the view that capitalism itself is the source of this strongest and ultimate alienation. In place of the Feuerbachian generic man, with his unchangingly abstract natural status, there is now a complex of social relationships changing in the course of history, and above all one characterized by class stratifications and antagonisms. To be sure, alienation includes both the exploiting class and the exploited, especially in capitalism as the strongest form of this self-alienation and objectification. "But," says *The Holy Family,* "the former class feels comfortable and confirmed in this self-alienation, knowing alienation to be *its own power* and possessing in it the appearance of a human existence. But the exploited class feels itself destroyed through alienation, in which it perceives its own impotence and the reality of an inhuman existence" (MEGA, I, 3, p. 206). The particular labor-divisive and class-based form of production and mode of exchange—above all the capitalist varieties— were shown to be the ultimate source of alienation.

Certainly from 1843 on, Marx was a materialist. *The Holy Family* gave birth to the materialistic conception of history and, with it, scientific socialism. The *Theses,* produced between *The Holy Family* of 1844-45 and *The German Ideology* of 1845-46, represent Marx's formal departure from Feuerbach, and the heir's highly original form of succession to his inheritance. Empirical political experience in his Rhine period plus Feuerbach rendered Marx immune to "spirit" [*Geist*]— even as construed by the left-Hegelian school. Having taken up the standpoint of the proletariat, Marx was able to search for the concrete cause, and was hence truly and fundamentally humanistic.

But of course the departure in this case was no complete break. Large areas of Marx's work, even after the farewell marked by the *Theses,* still offer evidence of a link with Feuerbach. Closest to the abandoned territory, even on purely chronological grounds, is *The German Ideology,* which follows directly on the *Theses.* Many a critical formulation of the *Theses* recurs here, albeit the criticism leveled against Feuerbach is quite different from the murderous annihilation of the third-rate Hegelians. Feuerbach was still part of bourgeois ideology, so that any involvement in controversy with its pseudo-radical disintegrative manifestations (for example, Bruno Bauer and Stirner) necessarily brought him into *The German Ideology.* Yet occasionally, Feuerbach himself is, so to speak, the handle of the decisive weapon of Marx's assault on him, and especially on the left-Hegelians. Accordingly, *The German Ideology* uses the name of Feuerbach and his critique of religion as a point of departure for a critique of a "supersession" of idealism that remained within the idealistic framework. "None of these philosophers thought of inquiring about the connection of German philosophy with German reality, or about the relation between its critique and its own material environment" (MEGA, I, 5, p. 10).

On the other hand, Marx emphasizes Feuerbach's "great merit by comparison with the 'pure' materialists in that he perceived that man too is a 'sensuous object'." Actually, the importance of Feuerbach for the development of Marxism is shown as much by the aforementioned recognition, as it is indicated negatively by Marx's criticism of his abstract and historical notion of man, which culminated in the un-Feuerbachian or even anti-Feuerbachian aspects of developed

Marxism. Marx recognized that without seeing man as a "sensuous object" it would have been far more difficult materialistically to see the human factor as the root of all social matters. That is, Feuerbach's *anthropological* materialism facilitated the transition from mere mechanical to historical materialism. Marx's criticism of Feuerbach was that, without the concretization of the human factor as involving persons actually existing, and above all, socially active, with real relationships to one another and to nature, materialism and history would have remained forever sundered, despite all "anthropology."

Nevertheless, for Marx, Feuerbach always remained significant, both as a transitional figure and as the only contemporary philosopher with whom argument was at all possible, and clarifying and productive into the bargain. The basic ideas to which Marx reacted critically, and beyond which he was to proceed productively, are contained in essence in Feuerbach's major work, *The Essence of Christianity* (1841). Other writings of Feuerbach that are relevant in this respect are his *Preliminary Theses toward the Reform of Philosophy* (1842), and the *Principles of the Philosophy of the Future* (1843). The earlier writings of the philosopher could scarcely have been important for Marx, seeing that, at least until 1839, Feuerbach was not sufficiently original, being too much under the influence of Hegel. Only after 1839 did Feuerbach apply the Hegelian concept of self-alienation to religion, and state that his first idea had been God, his second, reason, and his third and last, man. Just as the Hegelian rationalistic philosophy had superseded religious faith, so now philosophy was to put man, with nature as his basis, in place of Hegel. For all that, Feuerbach was unable to find a way to reality; and he discarded the most important element in Hegel, namely, the dialectical method. The *Theses* first pointed a way from what was only an anti-Hegel road onto one leading toward a new, alterable reality; away from the materialism of what might be termed the base behind the lines, toward an active front.

Arrangement of the Theses

The problem of the arrangement of the *Theses* is an old, yet also a new problem. Pedagogic suasions have influenced many attempts to change the order of the theses by grouping those that seem to belong together. On the other hand, the numerical sequence is sometimes left as it is, on the assumption that it is possible to organize the theses consecutively. A consecutive arrangement would produce something like the following result: Theses 1, 2, and 3 would be subsumed under "the unity of theory and practice in thought"; Theses 4 and 5 under "the understanding of reality in contradictions"; Theses 6, 7, 8, and 9 under "reality itself in contradictions"; Theses 10 and 11 under "the place and function of dialectical materialism in society."

This is an ordering according to numbers. But any classification of this type treats the series both too seriously, as though forever fixed, like the Roman Tables or the Decalogue, and too lightly and formalistically, like a series of postage stamps.

But numeration is not systematization, and Marx least of all requires such a substitute. The theses should be grouped in accordance with a philosophical and not an arithmetical pattern, that is, the sequence of the theses must be dictated by their themes and contents. So far as is known, there is as yet no commentary on the *Theses*. Yet only by the aid of one emerging from the common concern itself will the creative connection of the brevity and depth of the *Theses* become clear: first, an epistemological group relating to *perception* and *activity* (Theses 5, 1, and 3); second, an anthropological-historical group dealing with self-alienation, its *real cause and true materialism;* third, the synoptic or theory-practice group relating to *proof and confirmation* (Theses 2 and 8); last, the most important thesis, the *slogan* as a consequence of which the spirits not only finally depart, but cease to be anything other than spirits (Thesis 11). Appropriately, the epistemological group would properly open with Thesis 5, and the an-

63

thropological-historical one with Thesis 4—for these theses represent the two basic doctrines of Feuerbach, which Marx recognizes (relatively), and from which he moves forward in the remaining theses of the respective groups. The basic tenet accepted in Thesis 5 is the rejection of abstract thought, and that in Thesis 4 the rejection of human self-alienation. And, corresponding to the first principle of materialist dialectics signified here, between the individual theses within the respective groups there is a free movement of complementary voices; just as there is a permanent interchange of relationships between the groups: a cohesive and integral whole.

The Epistemological Group—Perception and Activity: Theses 5, 1, and 3

These propositions express the recognition that even in thinking one must start from sense data. Perception, and not the concept deduced from it, is the beginning by which all materialistic cognition expresses itself. It was Feuerbach who recalled attention to this fact at a time when every academic street corner still resounded with "spirit," "concept," and again "concept." Thesis 5 stresses this achievement: Feuerbach is "not satisfied" with cerebral existence: he wants his feet on the ground he is observing. Yet Thesis 5, and then, above all, Thesis 1, make clear that with a *contemplative* sensuousness (the only sort known to Feuerbach), the feet are not yet able to walk, and the ground itself remains impassable. Indeed, he who contemplates in this manner will not even try to move, and will remain set in a posture of satisfaction. Hence Thesis 5 teaches that mere perception "does not . . . conceive sensuousness as practical human sensuous activity." Furthermore, Thesis 1 reproaches all previous materialism for interpreting perception "only in the form of objects," "but not as *sensuous human activity, praxis,* not subjectively." So it appears that the active aspect of reality, in contrast to materialism, "was developed abstractly by idealism which, of course, does not

64

recognize real sensuous activity as such." In place of inert contemplation, the approach in which all previous materialism, including that of Feuerbach, persisted, there was now the factor of human activity, already within the process of sensuous and therefore immediate, basic-incipient cognition. Sensuousness as knowledge, as the real basis of knowledge, is therefore in no way the same as contemplative perception.

This emphasis of Thesis 1 on the *concept of activity* does indeed derive from idealistic epistemology, notably the particular form developed in the modern bourgeois period. This concept presupposed as its basis a society in which the ruling class saw or deserved to see itself in activity, that is, in labor—or at least would have liked to do so. But this holds true in capitalist society only to the extent that labor (or, more correctly, the *appearance* of labor round about the ruling class) is no longer shameful but actually honored, in contrast to all pre-bourgeois societies. This phenomenon results from the necessity of profits, from the productive forces released in this profit-oriented society. Labor, which in an ancient slaveholding society and in feudal serfdom was regarded as dishonorable (in Athens even sculptors were counted as members of the lower class), is understandably not reflected in the ideas of the ruling class, in this respect wholly in contrast to the ideology of the entrepreneur, the bourgeois, the so-called *homo faber*. The latter possessed a dynamics of profit which remained progressive for a long time, was liberated in the modern period, and built modern bourgeois history; it was clearly evident in the superstructure too, and activated the economic basis itself.

This appears in the ethical realm in the form of a so-called ethics of labor, and epistemologically in the form of a concept of activity and of a *logos* of work in the realm of cognition. The morality of work, preached especially by the Calvinists in the interest of the accumulation of capital, was a capitalistic *vita activa* which opposed aristocratic idleness and the *vita contemplativa* of the contemplative monastic and academic existence. Parallel to this was the transformed *logos* of work in the

65

cognitive realm whereby knowledge was defined as "production," a concept cspccially over-developed in bourgeois rationalism. The new view of knowledge was quite different from the ancient and even scholastic ideas of knowledge as mere reception, as sight, *visio,* or passive reflection as retained in the concept of *"theoria,"* in accordance with the original meaning of the word: *vision.* Hence even Plato—*cum grano salis*—is ultimately a contemplative sensualist. For no matter how ideal his vision may be, and how purely oriented to ideas, it is still essentially receptive seeing, and the thought process is consistently interpreted after the mode of sensuous perception. Indeed, even Democritus, the first great *materialist* and the leading one prior to Marx, is also within this ideology, which is alien to work and does not *reflect the labor process.* For he too interprets knowledge as only passive. Thought, by which he believed the truly real to become known, that is, the reality of the atoms together with their mechanism, is here explained solely through the impression made by minute though corresponding images *(eidola)* which detach themselves from the surface of things and flow into the perceiving and knowing subject. There is no difference whatever between Plato and Democritus, with respect to epistemological inactivity. Both theories of knowledge are products of a slaveholding society, which is evident in the absence of the despised labor activity from the philosophical superstructure. Paradoxically, rationalism, the *idealism* of the modern period, which has frequently moved a long way from Plato, still reflects the labor process in its epistemology much more strongly than the *materialism* of the modern period, which never deviated so much from Democritus, its classical progenitor. The serenely reflecting mirror, with its omission of the work process, is found much more frequently in materialist theory, including that of Feuerbach, than the fervor *(pathos)* of "production," let alone the dialectical reciprocal reflection of subject-object or object-subject.

Among the more modern materialists, only Hobbes teaches rational "production" with the basic proposition that remained valid until Kant: only those objects are knowable which can be construed mathematically. Yet although Hobbes, on the basis of this proposition, was able to define philosophy as the doctrine of the mathematic-mechanical motion of bodies and consequently as materialism, he was unable to discard the "form of the object" castigated by Marx; that is, he failed to go beyond merely contemplative materialism.

Another development took place within idealism where "production" passed over from *geometric construction* into the real work pattern of *historical genesis*. This for the first time happened decisively in Hegel. His *Phenomenology of the Spirit* first took seriously, from the perspective of *historical* idealism, the dynamics of the epistemological concept of labor. This seriousness also went far beyond the merely *mathematical-idealistic pathos* of production, which influenced the great rationalists of the period of manufactures (Descartes, Spinoza, and Leibniz) in their partial or total idealism. There is no better testimony to the importance of Hegel's *Phenomenology* (which Feuerbach never really understood) than Marx's comments in the *Economic and Philosophic Manuscripts,* where he interprets the real achievement of the *Phenomenology* as Hegel's "comprehension of the nature of labor and his understanding of objective man (true, because real, man) the product of his own labor" (MEGA, I, 3, p. 156). This statement best clarifies the alleged deficiency of merely contemplative materialism until and including Feuerbach: the earlier materialism had lacked that *permanently oscillating subject-object relationship which is known as labor.* For this reason Feuerbach still interpreted things, reality, and sensuous materiality only "in the form of objects" and apart from "sensuous human activity." By contrast, the standpoint of Hegel's *Phenomenology* was, as Marx said, that of modern political economy, whereas the epistemological position of Feuerbach was that of a slaveholding society or of serfdom, in the light of the inert and still contemplative character of his materialism.

Marx made it abundantly clear that bourgeois activity is not yet integral or just, and cannot be so, seeing that it is only the appearance of labor, inasmuch as the production of value is never accomplished by the entrepreneur himself, but by the peasant, the artisan, and finally the wage earner. Another reason is that the abstract, reified, and tortuous circulation of commodities in the free market allows only those relationships which are passive, external, and, ultimately, abstract. Hence Thesis 1 made the point that even the epistemological reflection of activity could be only abstract, since idealism, "of course, does not recognize real sensuous activity as such."

Yet even the bourgeois materialist Feuerbach, intent on breaking away from abstract thinking, and seeking real objects instead of reified concepts, omitted human activity from this real existence, and did not even interpret it as "objective activity." This thought is developed further in the Introduction to *The German Ideology:* "Feuerbach speaks in particular of the perception of natural science, and mentions mysteries which are revealed only to the eye of the physicist or chemist. Yet where would natural science be without industry and commerce? Even this 'pure' natural science first receives its purpose as well as its material through commerce and industry, and through the sensuous activity of men. So much is this activity, this continuous sensuous labor and creation, this production, the basis of the entire sensuous world, that were it interrupted for just one year, Feuerbach would not only discover a tremendous change in the natural world but would very soon be without the entire human world and his own capacity for perception, and indeed his own existence. In all this the priority of external nature certainly remains unquestioned, and all this has no application to the original men produced by *generatio aequivoca.* But this distinction is meaningful only to the extent that man is thought of as separate from nature. Moreover, this nature prior to human society is not the nature in which Feuerbach lives, not the nature which no longer exists anywhere today—except perhaps on some Australian coral islands of recent origin—and hence does not exist for Feuerbach" (MEGA, I, 5, pp. 33 ff.). These sentences stress the importance of human labor, unlocated as an object by Feuerbach, as perhaps the most important object in the world of man's environment.

Being, which determines everything, has men, who are themselves active, within it. The remarkable consequences of this fact make Thesis 3 particularly important in opposition not only to Feuerbach but to the vulgar Marxists. Two additional concepts of the "sensible world," a bad one and another that is frequently misunderstood, concern the empiricist favorites of the view (ostensibly remote from activity) which sees in "circumstances" only whatever lies about human beings. In this connection the so-called *"given circumstance"* is a particularly objective concept and thus one with an apparently materialist orientation. Yet apart from the fact that its meaning makes it an interchangeable concept that would have no validity were there no subject to whom alone something is or could be given, in the world which constitutes man's environment there is scarcely any given which would not equally be the product of some activity. For this reason Marx speaks of "material," which natural science first receives from commerce and industry. In fact, phenomena appear as "given" only to the superficial observer. A little penetration will show that every object in our normal surroundings is by no means a pure *datum*. An object is, rather, the final outcome of antecedent processes of human labor; and even the raw material, quite apart from the fact that it is completely transformed, has been drawn from the forest by labor or hewed out of the rocks, or improved after having been extracted from the depths of the earth.

The second proposition of so-called "non-active" perception begins with a wholly legitimate and indeed decisively materialistic concept, namely, *the priority of being to consciousness.* Epistemologically this priority expresses itself as the existence of an external world independent of human existence; and historically as a priority of the material basis to mind.

But here again Feuerbach has unilaterally stultified this

truth, or exaggerated it mechanically by omitting human activity here as well. The independence of being from consciousness, in the realm of normal human surroundings, is in no way the same as the independence of being from human labor.

Through the mediation of labor—with the external world, the independence of this world from consciousness—its objectivity is not eliminated, but actually achieves its final formulation. For just as human activity itself has an objective character, so the subject-object relationship, by virtue of the fact that it occurs, also constitutes a part of the external world. This external world also exists independently of consciousness in that it does not appear solely in the form of the subject; but, in addition, it does not appear only "in the form of the object."

Indeed, the external world represents a *reciprocal mediation of subject and object,* so that everywhere existence indeed does determine consciousness; but, on the other hand, historically decisive existence, that is, economic existence, everywhere comprises objective consciousness to an extraordinary extent.

Yet for Feuerbach all being is an autarchic *prius* as a purely pre-human basis—with nature as the base and man as just the flower and not as an intrinsic natural force. The human mode of production, the metabolism in conjunction with nature that occurs in and is regulated by the work process, and, indeed, the basis consisting of the conditions of production: all this possesses consciousness within itself. Similarly, the material base in every society is activated in turn by the consciousness superstructure.

As to reciprocal action in this being-consciousness relationship, Thesis 3 describes the priority of economic existence in a far from vulgar-materialist way, for it allows human consciousness, the most "real" of all places in the "conditions" or "circumstances" by putting it within the external world that it has helped to construct.

Mechanistic environmental theory asserts that "men are the

products of circumstances and education and therefore that transformed men are products of other circumstances and changed education." Against this one-sided and often wholly naturalistic doctrine of direct reflection (milieu equals soil, climate), Thesis 3 states "that circumstances are changed by men and that the educator himself has to be educated." This is a truth far superior to the conventional materialism of the past.

Of course, this does not mean that a change of this kind could occur without any reference to the objective lawfulness that applies equally to the subjective factor and activity factor. At this point Marx is waging a war on two fronts: against mechanistic environmental theory, which tends ultimately to fatalism, with regard to existence, and against the idealistic subject theory, which culminates in "putschism," or at least in excessive optimism with regard to activity. A passage in *The German Ideology* supports and supplements Thesis 3 along these lines, that is, on the basis of superlatively effective reciprocal motion of men and circumstances, and of a continuously reciprocal and dialectical subject-object mediation. Consequently, in history there is "at every stage a material result, a sum of productive forces, and an historically engendered relationship to nature and of individuals to one another, which are transmitted to each generation by its predecessor. This class of productive forces, capital resources, and circumstances may indeed be modified by the new generation, but also ordains the latter's own condition of life, giving it a definite development and a special character. Hence men are made by circumstances just as much as men make circumstances." Marx particularly stresses the reciprocity of subject and object at this point; and the relationship between circumstances and men is placed before its converse, but in such a way that man and his activity always remain the specific component of the material basis of history, and are actually its root, and therefore represent its transformability. According to Marx, even the idea (in theory) becomes a material force when it takes hold of the masses. Very clearly, the technico-political

71

transformation of circumstances is such a force; equally, when grasped thus, the subject factor remains within the material world.

Finally, the Third Thesis is further developed in *Capital* I, where man is quite decisively emphasized in relation to the external world, and, indeed, to Nature: "[Man] opposes himself to Nature as one of her own forces, setting in motion arms and legs, head and hands, the natural forces of his body, in order to appropriate Nature's productions in a form adapted to his own wants. By thus acting on the external world and changing it, he at the same time changes his own nature . . . The earth itself is an instrument of labor, but when used as such in agriculture implies a whole series of other instruments and a comparatively high development of labor."

Accordingly, human activity and consciousness are interpreted as a part of Nature, and indeed its most important part—as transformative praxis at the very basis of material existence, which in its turn primarily determines the ensuing consciousness.

The Feuerbach who had no revolutionary mandate, and who never went beyond a definition of man as a natural species being, had no sense of this increased primacy of Nature (increased, that is, by human activity). Ultimately, this is why history does not appear in Feuerbach's purely contemplative materialism, and why he never advanced beyond a contemplative attitude. He continued to view the object in an antiquated, "aristocratic" way, inconsistently and in contrast to his feeling for man, whom—once again only theoretically and as a mere flowering of extant Nature—he placed at the center of his critique of religion (but of no other). He therefore looked down at action from his lofty position, and saw it only as a sordid undertaking: "Active perception is a form of apprehension soiled and stained by egotism" (*The Essence of Christianity,* 1841). This is the sentence to which Marx refers in his First Thesis when he says that for Feuerbach, "practical activity is apprehended and fixed only in its dirty-Judaical manifestation." And how much arrogance of this sort appeared

72

later as perception increasingly "soiled and stained by egotism," coupled itself ideologically with a so-called *pure* perception, and then a so-called truth for its own sake. How
much "equestrian science" arose here, high-seated, *au dessus
de la melée* (apart from the dirt within it); how much aristoc-
racy of knowledge (without *aristoi*) sensibly foreswore the
grubbiness of praxis, and held itself aloof from what was right,
from *justice.*

With foresight, Marx opposes to this kind of utter misunderstanding (typified by Feuerbach's) the real fervor of "revolutionary, practical-critical activity." As a materialist Marx
emphasizes, precisely within being itself, the subjective factor
of productive activity, which is substantive in the same way as
the objective factor. Now, this has tremendous consequences
(even against vulgarized versions of Marxism) and makes this
section of the *Theses* particularly valuable. Unless the factor
of human labor is taken into consideration, the basic *prius* of
being, which is by no means a *factum brutum* or a given,
cannot be understood in human history. Certainly it cannot be
combined with the best form of activist perception, with which
Thesis 1 concludes, namely, "revolutionary, practical-critical
activity." The working man, the vital subject-object relationship which exists under all "conditions," belongs decisively, as
far as Marx is concerned, to the material basis; the subject
within the world is the world as well.

Anthropological-Historical Group—Self-Alienation and True Materialism: Theses 4, 6, 7, 9, and 10

In the human perspective, one must always start out from
alienation. Thesis 4 announces the theme: Feuerbach unveiled
self-alienation in its religious aspect. Hence this work con-
sisted in a resolution of the "religious world into its secular
basis." But Marx remarks that Feuerbach overlooked the fact
that after the completion of this task the main work still
remained to be done. As Thesis 6 states more clearly, Feuer-

bach had resolved the essence of religion into a secular basis, by reducing it to the essence of man. This was in itself a significant undertaking inasmuch as it took a sharp look at the role of human wishes. Feuerbach's "anthropological critique of religion" derived the entire transcendental realm from "wishful thinking"; the gods are the wishes of the human heart transformed into real beings. Similarly, this hypostatization of wishes brings about a duplication of the world as an imaginary as well as a real one, in which process man transfers his best essence from this mundane world into a transcendental one. It is therefore necessary to abolish this self-alienation, that is, to restore the heavens to mankind once more, by means of anthropological criticism and an investigation of origins.

This is where Marx's consistency enters upon the scene and refuses to stop with man when understood as an abstract genus, without specific articulation as to class and history. Feuerbach, who had so severely criticized Hegel for his reification of concepts, did localize his abstract genus of man empirically, but only in a form permitting it to dwell within the single individual, apart from society, apart from social history. For this reason, Thesis 6 emphasizes: "But the essence of man is no abstraction inherent in each particular individual. In its reality the essence of man is the totality of social relations."

Indeed, with his empty connection between the particular individual and the abstract *humanum* (omitting society) Feuerbach is little more than a latter-day descendent of the Stoa and its sequelae in natural law and in the ideas of toleration in modern bourgeois times. The Stoic morality too had been restricted to private individuals after the decline of the Greek *polis*. As Marx said in his doctoral dissertation: "Thus the nocturnal moth, when the universal sun has gone down, seeks the lamplight of a private world" (MEGA, I, 1/1, p. 133).

On the other hand, within the Stoa, by eliding all national-societal relationships, the abstract genus man was made to stand out over and above the single individual as the uniquely universal being, as the locus of *communis opinio* and of *recta ratio,* at all times and among all peoples; that is, as the

74

universal home of man arranged within the equally universally valid world residence. Only this house of mankind was not the vanished *polis* but it was half (with a serviceable ideology) the Pax Romana, the cosmopolitan *imperium* of Rome; and half (with an abstract utopia) a fraternal brotherhood of human individuals who had found wisdom. It was not without reason, therefore, that the concept of *humanitas,* both as a generic and a value concept, developed at the court of the young Scipio, with the Stoic Panaitios as its founder.

Hence Feuerbach, with his abstract genus man, has primarily taken up neo-Stoicism, in its modern bourgeois manifestation, with an empty connection between the individual and the generality, as evident as the abstract elevated concept of the *citoyen* and the Kantian enthusiasm for a universal humanity that reflected the *citoyen* notion in a German-moralistic fashion. Of course, the individuals of the modern period were now capitalists, rather than Stoic private pillars; and their *universal* was not the classical *Oekumene,* which was to extinguish the diversity of peoples, but an idealization of the ancient *polis*— the generality of bourgeois human rights, with the abstract *citoyen* at the head as a moral-humane species ideal.

Nevertheless, there are important economically determined correspondences here (otherwise neo-Stoicism would not have existed in the seventeenth and eighteenth centuries). In both sectors, society is atomized into individuals, and in both an abstract genus and an abstract ideal of mankind, humanitarianism is elevated above them. Marx criticizes this very abstraction raised over mere individuals, and defines the essence of humanity as "the totality of social relations." Hence Thesis 6 is directed both against Feuerbach's ahistorical consideration of mankind as such, and also against something else related to it—the purely anthropological generic concept of this mankind, as a generality binding together many individuals in a purely biological manner. Marx retains the value concept of humanity so clearly evident in Thesis 10. The expression "real humanism" with which the introduction to *The Holy Family* begins is abandoned in *The German Ideology,* to be sure,

75

together with every vestige of bourgeois democracy, for the proletarian revolutionary standpoint has been attained, and dialectical-historical materialism has been born. Yet Thesis 10 still proclaims, with all the emphasis on value of a humanistic opposition, and hence of a "real humanism" (one which would exist and be enabled to hold only in a socialist form): "The standpoint of the older type of materialism is civil society; the standpoint of the new materialism is human society or socialized humanity."

The human factor [*das Humanum*] is not present everywhere in every society "as an inner, mute general quality which unites the many individuals in a purely natural way." Indeed, it does not reside in any sort of extant generality but is to be found only in difficult process, and as such comes to fruition only together with Communism.

For this very reason, the new proletarian standpoint does not eliminate the value concept of humanism. On the contrary, it alone allows that concept to be realized for the first time. The more scientific socialism is, the *more concrete is the concern for man at its center,* and the more certain is the real elimination *of his self-alienation as its goal;* not after the fashion of Feuerbach, as an *abstract genus,* with all too excessively exalted human and sacramental elements.

Accordingly, Marx takes up in Thesis 9, above all, the theme of the epistemological group of theses, directed against Feuerbach's anthropology. "The highest point attained by contemplative materialism—materialism, that is, which does not conceive sensuousness as practical activity—is the contemplation of particular individuals and of civil society." Thus a class barrier is finally noted, the same one that impedes revolutionary *activity* in Feuerbach's epistemology, and now, in his anthropology, impedes *history and society.* Marx's development of Feuerbach's anthropology as a criticism of religious self-alienation is therefore not only a matter of consistency but is an extension of demythization—notably of Feuerbach himself and of anthropological fetishism. Thus Marx advances from a generalized ideal type man, beyond mere individuals, to the basis of real humanity and possible humaneness.

It was necessary to examine as well the processes which are really at the root of alienation. Men have duplicated their world not only because they have a riven consciousness, infused with desires, but far more because this consciousness, together with its reflection in religion, corresponds to a birfurcation which is much closer at hand, namely, that within society. It is social relationships themselves which are torn and sundered, which reveal bottom and top layers, and struggles between these classes and murky ideologies held by the superordinate group, of which the religious is only one among many. To Marx, it appeared that the work which primarily remained to be done was to find this more proximate aspect of the secular foundation—a veritable this-worldly basis, in contrast to Feuerbach's abstract-anthropological one. The latter, alien to history and undialectical, had no understanding of this point, but Thesis 4 crystallizes it: "But the fact that the secular basis separates itself from itself and establishes an independent realm for itself in the clouds can be explained only by the self-cleavage and self-contradictions of this secular basis. Therefore, the latter must be understood in its contradictions and revolutionized in practice. Thus, for example, once the earthly family is discovered to be the secret of the holy family, the former must itself be destroyed both in theory and in practice."

It follows that criticism of religion, in order to be truly radical (which according to Marx's definition means a grasping of things at their root [*radix*]), demands a criticism of the mundane relationships basic to the celestial ones—their misery, their contradictions, and their false and imaginary resolution of the contradictions. As early as 1844, in his Introduction to *A Critique of Hegel's Philosophy of Right,* Marx had given this thrilling formulation, which cannot possibly be misunderstood: "Criticism of religion ends . . . with a categorical imperative to overthrow all conditions in which man is a degraded, enslaved, abandoned, and contemptible being" (MEGA, I, 1/1, pp. 614 ff.).

Only after such progressive criticism, followed by its practical revolutionary implications, would a condition be reached that would no longer need illusions either as deception or as substitute: "Criticism has plucked the imaginary flowers from the chain, not so that man can bear the chain without fantasy or consolation, but so that he can throw off the chain and pluck the living flower" (MEGA, I, 1/1, p. 608). To achieve the last-named ends, it would be necessary first for the earthly family to be disclosed as the secret of the celestial one, by moving in the direction of that mature economic-materialistic "secret science" which later prompted Marx to say in his *Capital* (I): "It requires very little acquaintance, for example, with the history of the Roman Republic, in order to realize that the history of the landed estates constitutes its secret history." Consequently, the analysis of religious self-alienation, if it is to be truly radical, must go beyond ideologies to the analysis of the proximate role of the State, and then on to political economy, where it will finally reach the real "anthropology": a fundamental insight, based on the social sciences, into the "relationship of man to other men and to nature."

By virtue of the fact, pointed out in Thesis 7, "that the 'religious sentiment' is itself a social product," the process of production cannot and must not be forgotten because of the product—which is what Feuerbach, in his unhistorical and undialectical orientation, had done. It is to this inadequacy of Feuerbach's untenable analysis that the following passage in *Capital* refers: "Actually, it is much easier to find by analysis the earthly core of the religious nebulous duplications in the clouds than, conversely, to *develop* from any particular realistic conditions of life their transcendentalized forms in the sky. The latter is the uniquely materialistic method and therefore the scientific one. The defects inherent in any abstract natural-scientific materialism that omits the historical process are readily apparent in the abstract and ideological notions of their spokesmen, once the latter go beyond their own specialty." In

78

The German Ideology, Marx adds a comment clarifying the basic difference between dialectical-historical materialism and the older mechanistic type: "Insofar as Feuerbach is a materialist, history does not exist for him, and insofar as he considers history, he is no materialist." Feuerbach himself expressed this notion in another way, namely, that he looked back, as a materialist (that is, in his view of the natural basis), but forward as an idealist (that is, in regard to ethics and the philosophy of religion). It is precisely the omission of society, and of history and its dialectics, from Feuerbach's materialism, and the resulting failure to include problems of life in the old mechanical materialism, which was the only one known to him, that made this philosopher's idealism confused. This becomes obvious in his ethical doctrine, and in various aspects of his thought which verge on Sunday-school uplift. Once again, what is evident is, as Thesis 9 puts it, "the contemplation of particular individuals and of civil society"; and once again it is clear that Feuerbach's apparent disposal of *religion* has in effect only derived it anthropologically, but has not criticized it sociologically. All that he has done is not to criticize the contents of religion but only their transposition into another world beyond, and the consequential weakening of man and his mundane existence. Insofar as Feuerbach wished to remind human nature of its squandered wealth, there were problems in such a reduction. For who would overlook the profound humanity or the humanity of profundity in art suffused with religion, as—say—in Giotto, Grünewald, Bach, and even Bruckner? Yet Feuerbach, with incomparable humanity, fraternal feeling, and sensitivity, turns all this into a sort of non-denominational *"pectoral theology."* Moreover, he retains in the inevitable emptiness of his "forward-looking idealism" practically all the attributes of his Father-God, so to speak, as virtues in themselves, omitting only the concept of a Father-God. Instead of "God is merciful," or "God is love," "is all-powerful," "performs miracles," and "hears prayers," the new formulation is, so to say: "Mercifulness, love, omnipotence, the performance of miracles and the hearing of prayers—these are divine." The entire theological apparatus remains in tact except that it is transferred from its celestial site to some abstract locality, with the reified virtues of a "basis in nature." But this did not produce a problem of the humanistic heritage of religion, which is what Feuerbach clearly had in mind. Instead, what resulted now was cut-rate religion in the interest of habit-ridden Philistines whose disillusionment with religion was incomplete and faulty. Engels was justified in indicating the stale crumbs of religion in Feuerbach's thought.

By contrast, in its view of religion Marxism is no "forward-oriented idealism," but a forward-oriented materialism; it is a full materialism without an inadequately demythized heaven which it is necessary to introduce upon earth. The truly total explanation of the world in terms of itself, which is termed dialectical-historical materialism, also presupposes the transformation of the world from itself—into another world of difficulties, which has nothing whatever to do with a mythological other world or its Lord or Father.

The Theory-Practice Group—Proof and Verification: Theses 2 and 8

Here thought is not held to be pale and powerless. Thesis 2 sets it above sensuous perception or contemplation, with which and at which it merely begins. Feuerbach had a poor opinion of thought, because it led from the particular to the general. But, for Marx, thought by no means aims solely at the pure general and abstract, but, on the contrary, plainly includes the mediated and essential connections of any phenomenon, something still hidden in the merely sensuous aspects of the phenomenon. Hence thought, which Feuerbach admits only as abstract, because of its mediating character, is really concrete; indeed, it is precisely the merely sensuous that is abstract when unaccompanied by thought. Of course, thought must lead back to perception in order to prove itself by

80

it, when perception has been permeated by this thought; but such perception is by no means the passive and unmediated something Feuerbach would have it be. The proof can more readily be found only in the intermediation of the perception, that is, only in that sensuousness which has been worked over in theory and which has become a "thing for us" [*Ding für uns*]. But this is ultimately the sensuousness of a praxis mediated and achieved by theory. Hence the function of thought, much more so than sensuous perception, is an activity that is critical, penetrating, interpretative—and the best proof of this is the practical effort at such revelation. Just as all truth is a truth in regard to something, and there is no such thing as a truth existing only for itself (except as self-deception or mere musing), so there is no full proof of a truth from itself as a truth that remains purely theoretical. In other words, there is no *possible theoretically immanent* full proof; only a partial one is practicable in a purely theoretical manner, as is still the case for the most part in mathematics. Yet even here, it is partial and specific, for it does not actually go beyond mere inner "consistency" and logically consequent "correctness." However, correctness is not yet truth, the reflection of reality *and* the power to exert an influence upon reality, in keeping with its recognized potentialities and laws. In other words, truth is not just a relationship in theory but is wholly *a relationship in both theory and practice.* Thesis 2: "The question of whether human thinking can arrive at objective truth is not a theoretical but a practical question. Man has to prove the truth, that is, the reality and power, the 'this-sidedness' of his thinking, in practice. The dispute over the reality or non-reality of thinking which is isolated from practice is a purely scholastic exercise."

This means that the dispute is a scholastic one, if one assumes a closed immanence of thought (including mechanistic materialistic thought); indeed, such a contemplative academy had been the location of all previous concepts of truth. By virtue of the relationship of theory and practice, Thesis 2 is quite original and new; in contrast, "all previous" philosophy appears "scholastic." Ancient and medieval epistemology did

81

not reflect human activity; and bourgeois-abstract activity was not truly mediated with its object. Both at the time of the ancient and medieval contempt for labor, and at the time of the bourgeois ethic of work (but without the concreteness of labor), practical activity—technical or political—appeared as at best the "application" of theory, and not as an attestation of theory as concrete—which is the case with Marx; nor yet as the key reapplied as a lever of true reflection for the purpose of an existentially apt praxis.

Thus in the end the right thought becomes identical with doing what is right. Activity, including one's partisan political stance, is present within thought from the start, and consequently appears at the end as the correct conclusion. The color of the decision in this conclusion is its own and not something brought in subsequently from outside. Study of the history of philosophy confirms the newness of the contribution of the theory-practice relationship, in contrast to any mere "application" of theory. This is clearly true even when a part of the theory intended action, as was the case with Socrates, and therefore with Plato, who sought to construct his utopia in Sicily, and also Stoicism, with logic as the mere wall, physics the tree, but ethics as the fruit. This is true also of Augustine, the local founder of the medieval papal Church, and of William of Occam at the end of the Middle Ages—the nominalistic destroyer of the papal Church in the interests of the rising national States. Behind all of these there was undoubtedly a practical mandate from society, yet theory led its own abstract life, and had no links with practice. It permitted itself only to descend to an "application" to practice, as a prince might condescend to his people, or—at best—an idea to its evaluation. This is true even of Bacon, in the precise bourgeois-practical utilitarianism of the modern period. Admittedly, he taught that knowledge is power and sought a new basis for all science, which he oriented as an *ars inveniendi*. Nevertheless, despite all his opposition to purely theoretical and contemplative knowledge, science did remain autonomous, and only its method was to be altered—in the direction of the inductive procedure of the methodically arranged experiment. Yet proof did not lie in practical activity, which even for him still appeared to be only the fruit and reward of truth, not its final criterion and demonstration.

The numerous "philosophies of the act" which arose out of Fichte and Hegel, and then returned to Fichte in the left-Hegelian school, were even more distant from the Marxist criterion or practical activity. Fichte's concept of the act itself did indeed show strength and consistency at certain important points of national policy, but ultimately vanished into thin air. The final service that it rendered was not so much to improve the world of the non-ego by working with it, but rather to eliminate it completely. What was demonstrated, so to speak, in this "praxis" that was basically hostile to the world was the subjective starting point of Fichtean ego idealism, but not an objective truth which comes into being only with and in the world.

It was Hegel in his *Phenomenology* who actually came nearest to developing a criterion for praxis, and this he did, significantly, on the basis of the work relationship. Moreover, Hegel's psychology features a transition from "theoretical mind" (perception, imagination, thought) to its antithesis, "practical mind" (feeling, drive, happiness), from which the "free mind" or "free spirit" would result synthetically. This synthesis was claimed to be the knowing will which, as will, thinks and knows itself—and finally, in the "rational State," wills what it knows, and knows what it wills.

Similarly, Hegel's *Logic* already demonstrates a super-ordination of the "practical idea" over the "ideal of considered cognition" [*Idee des betrachteten Erkennens*], insofar as "not only the worth of what is universal, but that of actuality pure and simple" pertains to what is good in practice (*Werke* V, pp. 320 f.). Lenin noted that "everything in the chapter on the 'Idea of cognition' . . . which clearly shows that practical activity is, for Hegel, an essential link in the analysis of the cognition process . . . forms a direct connection with Hegel when Marx introduces the criterion of practical activity into epistemology—see his *Theses on Feuerbach" (Posthumous Philosophical Writings)*. Nevertheless, at the end of his *Logic,* and at the end of his *Phenomenology* and his developed system, Hegel leads the world (thing, object, and substance) back into the subject, almost in the same way as Fichte, so that in the final analysis it is not praxis but recollection that crowns truth—the "science of manifest knowing"—and nothing more. It will also be recalled that Hegel has a famous remark at the end of the Introduction to his *Philosophy of Right,* to the effect that "philosophy always comes too late. As the *idea* of the world it first appears at a time when reality has completed its process of formation and is in a finished state." Thus, the closed cyclical thinker, the repository or the irremovable given, ultimately overcame the dialectical process-thinker and his crypto-praxis.

In order to assess the originality of Marx's theory of praxis, even in the environment of his youth, we must now consider the "praxis" of the Hegelian left. This was "the weapon of criticism," the so-called "philosophy of the act," at the time of Marx's youth. Yet this was essentially only a regress from the objective idealism of Hegel to the subjective type of Fichte— as demonstrated by Feuerbach himself with respect to Bruno Bauer. The so-called "philosophies of the act" were introduced by Cieszkowski's otherwise not valueless work of *Prolegomena to Historiosophy* (1838). Cieszkowski stated expressly that it was necessary to use philosophy to effect changes in the world. Indeed, the *Prolegomena* calls for a rational investigation of historical trends, in order to ensure proper action and, in particular, the making of world history through conscious and not instinctive deeds. In this way, Cieszkowski taught, the will would be brought to the same height to which Hegel had brought reason, so that— ultimately—praxis would be important not only before theory but after it. Although this sounds very significant, it remained an assertion without any consequence in Cieszkowski's later works; indeed, the "interest of the future" became for him increasingly irrational and obscure. His renunciation of specu-

84

lation became a renunciation of reason; activity became "active intuition," and his entire orientation toward the future culminated in an Amen-theosophy in the orthodox Church, pronounced at the time of the *Communist Manifesto.*

Finally, in Marx's own circle there was still Bruno Bauer, who also proclaimed a "philosophy of the act," and even one of world judgment, which was in fact the most subjective of all. When the reaction under Friederich Wilhelm IV put this "weapon of criticism" to the test, it produced in Bruno Bauer a retreat to individualism, and indeed to an egocentricity, contemptuous of the masses. Bauer's "critical criticism" was simply a tournament of and between ideas, a sort of art-for-art's-sake praxis of an arrogant mind or spirit with itself, which led ultimately to Stirner's *The Ego and Its Own.* Marx himself spoke the decisive word on this subject in *The Holy Family* in regard to his own major idea of authentic practical activity and its unique orientation of the goal of revolutionary practice. It would start with the proletariat, equipped with what was fruitful in Hegelian dialectics, and not with abstractions from the "faded and widowed Hegelian philosophy" (MEGA, I, 3, p. 189), let alone from Fichtean subjectivism. Fichte, that virtuous and angry man, did sometimes consider certain dynamic possibilities—in works ranging from *The Autonomous Commercial State* to the *Addresses to the German Nation.* He had expelled the French from German philosophy; nevertheless, his "critical criticism" traveled solely in the carriage of self-consciousness.

Coming closer to Marx, even that thoroughly honest socialist Moses Hess interpreted human action in such a way that it appeared to be separate from societal activity and to be reduced to a reform of the moral consciousness, a "philosophy of the act" without a developed economic theory behind it or a timetable showing a dialectically conceptualized trend. Thus the concepts of praxis before Marx are completely different from his conception of theory and praxis, from his theory of the unity between theory and practical activity. Instead of being merely attached to theory, so that thought, purely from the point of view of science, does not need to be "applied" and theory carries on its own autonomous life and its immanent self-sufficiency, in proof as well, in the view of Marx and of Lenin, theory and practice always oscillate toward one another. By virtue of the fact that both are mutually and reciprocally intermediated, practical activity presupposes theory, even as praxis itself releases and requires new theory for the progress of some new praxis. The concrete idea has never been more highly valued, for here it becomes the illumination for the act; nor has the act ever been more highly valued, for here it becomes the crown of truth.

At the same time, thought, because it assists, is thoroughly suffused with warmth—with the desire to be helpful, with love for victims, and with hatred for exploiters. These feelings make partisanship possible, without which no true knowledge accompanied by good deeds would be possible for socialism. Yet a feeling of love which is not illuminated by knowledge tends to inhibit the helping act which it longs for. It may all too easily become satisfied with its own virtue, and so become the mist of a new pseudo-active self-consciousness. In such a case, the result would not be the art-for-art's-sake criticism of Bruno Bauer, but a sentimental and uncritical criticism characterized by vagueness, as in Feuerbach himself, who always used, instead of praxis, his own ambivalent term *"Empfindung"* (sentiment). He reduced love to a generalized sentimental relationship between an I and a Thou, and revealed his lack of any social insight at this point by his retreat to isolated individuals and a gooey relationship between them. In this way, he effeminized humanity: "The new philosophy is in relation to its basis [!] actually nothing other than the essence of sentiment brought to consciousness. It affirms only in and with reason what every man—the real man—affirms in his heart" (*Werke* II, 1846, p. 324). This remark from the *Principles of the Philosophy of the Future* is in truth a substitution for action that was derived from the past, one that was Philistine, Papist, and, indeed, very often given to hypocrisy and sabotage.

It is the fault of the abstract and declamatory love of man

proclaimed in the past that there failed to emerge any willingness really to change the world in the direction of the good—and only a desire to perpetuate it in its evil state. Feuerbach's caricature of the Sermon on the Mount excluded any sort of hardness from the removal of injustice, but included every kind of laxity in the class struggle; this is the very reason why a generalized love—"socialism"—is welcomed by the crocodile tears of a philanthropy involved with capitalism. This is why Marx and Engels said: "They would preach the kingdom of love in opposition to a rotten actuality and hatred . . . but when experience shows that this love has not been effective in 1800 years, has not changed social relationships and has not been able to build its kingdom, then it clearly follows that this love which has been unable to overcome hatred does not offer the dynamic power needed for social reforms. This love is consumed in sentimental assertions which cannot remove any actual conditions; it merely acts as a soporific on those whom it feeds with its sentimental mash. Need gives men power: whosoever must help himself will do so. Consequently, it is the real conditions of this world, the sharp contrast in contemporary society between capital and labor, between bourgeoisie and proletariat, appearing in their most developed forms in industrial intercourse, which constitute the other strongly bubbling source of the socialist world view and the demand for social reforms . . . This iron necessity creates for socialist aspirations a wide dissemination and energetic followers; by transforming contemporary relationships, it will clear the way for social reforms more readily than all the love glowing in all the sentimental hearts in the world" (*Circular Letter against Kriege* [a disciple of Feuerbach], May 11, 1846).

Since then, what Thomas Münzer termed not only "fictional faith" but "fictional love" has spread more widely among renegades and pseudo-socialists than in Feuerbach's relatively harmless times. Their simulated love of mankind is only the martial weapon of an even more total hatred—namely, that directed against Communism. Indeed, this newly fictionized love exists only for the sake of war. It is accompanied by a mysticism, which was not absent from Feuerbach, to be sure, but which now purports to be a "progressive idealism." In the formless blustering of its emotionalism, and its anthropological reworking of the God-the-Father theme, this mysticism was no more inadequate than the above-mentioned poorly secularized and non-religious Philistinism.

But the mysteries of the pseudo-profound prattle of today's mysticism, no longer idealistic, are as different from Feuerbach's mysticism as his from that of Eckhart—making the heart murderous, and replacing the vacuous roseate mist with a nothingness to be exploited by the bourgeoisie. Thesis 8 says: "All the mysteries which lead theory to mysticism find their rational solution in human practice and in the comprehension [that is, the rational solution] of this practice." Here, of course, two kinds of mysteries are differentiated: those which represent the unexplained, the dilemmas, the jungle of the as yet uncomprehended contradiction within reality; and on the other hand, those properly termed "mysticisms," which represent idolatry of the darkness for its own sake.

Yet even things that as yet seem unintelligible, even the fog-clouds in them, can lead to mysticism; for this very reason, rational practice is the only human solution and the only rational solution is human practice—action which takes its stand on humanity, not the jungle. It should be noted too that the word "mysticism" is employed (not without reason) by Marx in regard to Feuerbach, and used to characterize the "non-sword" of love that leaves Gordian knots as they are.

To recapitulate: Feuerbach's mysteries, the love mysteries sans clarity, certainly have nothing in common with the rot and nocturnal irrationality that appeared later. Feuerbach stood on the German line of salvation that led from Hegel to Marx— even as there is a German line of doom that stretches from Schopenhauer to Nietzsche and their sequelae. Moreover, love for mankind, insofar as it clearly understands itself as directed toward the exploited, and progresses toward true knowledge, is unquestionably an indispensable factor in socialism. But if salt can lose its savor, sugar can do so much more easily; and if sentimental Christians can remain defeatist, this fate can all the more readily overtake sentimental socialists, in their hypocritical treason.

For this reason, Marx criticizes Feuerbach for a dangerous turgidity which (whatever else it might be) is ultimately a *"pectoral activity"* which brings about the very opposite of what is intended in its alleged altruism and unutterable universal love. Without a polarization in the love, without an equally concrete pole of hate, there is no true love. Without the partisanship of the revolutionary class standpoint there is only a "retrogressive idealism" and not a praxis that moves ahead. Without the primacy of the human intellect directed to action all the way, there are only mysteries of dissolution instead of a dissolution of mysteries. Hence the ethical conclusion of Feuerbach's philosophy of the future lacks both philosophy and future. Marx's theory-for-the-sake-of-practice set both in operation: thus ethics finally becomes flesh.

The Slogan and Its Significance: Thesis 11

It is recognized here that what is to come is closest and most important—but not in the wholly inadequate manner of Feuerbach, who from start to finish remains satisfied with a contemplation which leaves things as they are; or—even worse—believes it impossible to set about changing things—unless in a book. Of this the world takes no notice, because the world can so easily be inverted in false representations, that all reality is absent from the book. Every step outward would then be harmful to this introverted book living in its own idyllic preserve and disturb the autonomous life of factitious ideas. Yet even excellent books and theories which are true to their theme frequently show that typical contemplative pleasure and contentment in remaining in some limited context which once seemed functionally successful. As a result, such books and ideas actually fear any possible alteration of the world as represented, that might arise from them, because then the work—even when it itself establishes principles of the *future* (as in the case of Feuerbach)—would no longer be able to swoop and hover so freely through the ages.

If (as in the case of Feuerbach) a calculated or naïve political indifference is also in evidence, then the public is altogether confined to the reader—who is also a mere object of contemplation, no claim being made on his arms and action. Even though the standpoint may be a new one, it remains a mere observation post that offers no advice in regard to action. This is the sense of Marx's famous Eleventh Thesis: "The philosophers have only interpreted the world in different ways; the point is to change it." The difference from *every* previous motivation for thought is striking.

I have already remarked that brief propositions sometimes appear more readily intelligible than they really are. And famous propositions (though very much against their intention) sometimes fail to provoke thought, or are liable to be swallowed without being thoroughly chewed over. In such cases they occasionally produce problematic reactions, hostile to intellect, or at least alien to it, that could not possibly be more remote from the intention and meaning of the assertion in question. In the light of this finding, we must search for the exact intention of Marx's Eleventh Thesis—the proposition of a theoretician who was always attentive to philosophic precision.

It must not be misconstrued, or—more correctly—misapplied, by confusing it in any way with *pragmatism,* which derives from an area altogether remote from Marxism and, indeed, alien to it, spiritually inferior and—ultimately—wholly evil. Nevertheless, "busybodies" (as they say in America) are constantly latching on to Marx's thesis, as though it were identical with American cultural barbarism. The basis of American pragmatism is the view that truth is essentially nothing more than the social utility of ideas. There is supposed to be a sort of "aha-experience" of truth, when and insofar as it aims at a certain practical success, and shows itself actually capable of achieving it. With William James (*Pragmatism*, 1907) the businessman, as the "American way of life," still retains a certain universal humanity, seems almost human, and has the trimmings of a, so to speak, life-enhancing optimism about him. This is so because of the rosy packaging that it was still possible to present American capitalism in at the time, but above all because of the tendency of every class society to assert that its special interest is that of all mankind. For this reason, pragmatism at first purported to be a patron of these various interchangeable logical "instruments," by means of which the businessman of the higher order aims at successful "human relations." But there are few humane businessmen: even fewer than there are Marxist worldlings. Consequently, after James, pragmatism in America and throughout the bourgeoisie of the world soon revealed itself in its true colors: as the ultimate agnosticism of a society denuded of any will to truth. Two imperialistic wars (the first, that of 1914-1918, one of general imperialism; the second characterized by the partial imperialism of Nazi aggressors) enabled pragmatism to become a mature horse-trading ideology. Henceforth, there was to be no more concern for truth, not even as an "instrument" to be cultivated; and the roseate packaging of "successful human relations" went completely to the devil (who was present in it from the beginning). Henceforth, ideas would oscillate and fluctuate like stock issues, depending on war or business conditions—until finally the scandalous pragmatism of the Nazis appeared. Now right was defined as whatever served the interests of the German people (that is, German finance capital), while truth was defined as whatever served life (that is, maximum profit), or appeared to be of use to it. Such, when the time was ripe, were the consequences of pragmatism—however inoffensive or deceptive it might have seemed in terms of theory and praxis. Here a truth was apparently rejected for its own sake, and no admission was made that this was done for the sake of a lie, in the interests of business. In a pseudo-concrete manner, here too truth was deceptively required to be verified in practice, and even in

91

terms of a "transformation" of the world. The possibility of debasing Marx's Eleventh Thesis is immense as far as those who hold the intellect cheap and the pseudo-activists are concerned. Of course, from a moral viewpoint, these trumpery activists of the socialist movement have nothing to do with the pragmatists. Their will is pure, their goal revolutionary, their purpose humane. Yet, because they omit the intellect in all this, and consequently omit the entire richness of Marxist theory together with a critical acquisition of the entire cultural heritage within it, all this trial-and-error method, mechanical diddling, and pseudo-practicality features that terrible adulteration of Thesis 11 which is methodically so reminiscent of pragmatism. This addiction to a practicality bordering on pragmatism results from a form of falsification that even now has not been fully comprehended—yet ignorance of a result is no protection against stupidity. These "practicists" with their at best short-term credit for theory—particularly for complex theory—produced, in the very midst of Marxist illumination, the darkness of their own private ignorance and of a *ressentiment,* which is so easily combined with ignorance.

Sometimes it is not even pseudo-practicality, but some activity that lies behind this sort of antipathy to theory; the rigidity of anti-intellectualism also lives off its own destructive, inactive anti-philosophy. But this would be the less able to find support in the most precious of the Theses on Feuerbach, for then misunderstanding would have become blasphemy. Therefore, it must again be emphasized that *for Marx an idea is not true because it is useful, but useful because it is true.* In his essay "The Three Sources and Three Component Parts of Marxism" (1913), Lenin expressed it thus: "The doctrine of Marx is omnipotent because it is true." And he goes on to say: "It is the rightful successor to the best that man produced in the nineteenth century, in the form of German philosophy, British political economy, and French socialism." Previously he had remarked that "the genius of Marx consists precisely in his having supplied answers to questions already posed by the foremost human minds." In other words, realistic action within the world cannot be implemented without first consulting progressive theory—in economics and in philosophy. Hence, insofar as there was a lack of socialist theoreticians, there has always been a danger of losing contact with reality; for reality must not be interpreted schematically or simplistically if any practical activity on behalf of socialism is to succeed. The doors have been kept open by reason of the anti-pragmatism of the greatest intellectual interpreters of practical activity, because they are the witnesses to truth; but these doors may be shut at any time through an erroneous interpretion of Thesis 11, based on a pragmatic interest. In a grotesque fashion, Thesis 11, the highest triumph of philosophy, is thought to allow an abrogation of philosophy, a sort of non-bourgeois pragmatism. This does not serve the cause of the future, for the future will not arrive for us unless we comprehend it, and—conversely—unless our activist knowledge advances toward it as well. Reason (*ratio*) watches over this part of the course of praxis, even as it does over every path of the return to human decency—against the irrationality which ultimately shows itself in every practical action that lacks the guidance of conceptual thought. For if the destruction of reason sinks back into barbaric irrationality, then indifference to reason ends up in stupidity—which may not shed blood, to be sure, but will certainly ruin Marxism. *Hence banality too is tantamount to counter-revolution against Marxism itself—which is the implementation* (not the Americanization) *of the most progressive thought of mankind.*

So much, then, regarding false understanding, no matter where it arises. Yet what is false also needs illumination, precisely because Thesis 11 is *the most important—corruptio optimi pessima.* Moreover, because this Thesis is the most compressed, a commentary on it must pay more attention to its actual phrasing. What, then, is the implication of the words here, and what is the apparent antithesis between knowing and changing the world? There is no opposition, and, indeed, in the original, the word "but" (*"aber"*—which here suggests amplification, not opposition) is lacking (cf. MEGA, I, 5, p. 535), nor is there anything to suggest an "either/or." The philosophers of the past are reproached for having only *interpreted* the world differently, or more precisely, they are made aware of the existence of a class barrier in their enterprise. They are not, however, reprimanded for having philosophized. Yet, inasmuch as interpretation is akin to contemplation, and derives from it, non-contemplative knowledge is here singled out as the new variety that will truly carry the banner to victory. But the banner is still that of *knowledge,* which Marx has raised above his major work of learned research, although he allies it with action, not contemplative quiet. This major work replete with directives for action is termed *Capital,* however, not "Directions for Success" or "Propaganda of the Act." It contains no antecedent recipes for swift heroic action *ante rem,* but on the contrary stands in the midst of what is happening (*in re*), devoting conscientious research and philosophical investigation to the context of the most difficult aspects of reality. It stresses comprehended necessity and knowledge of the dialectical laws of evolution in both nature and society. Thus the first part of the proposition in Thesis 11 is directed exclusively against philosophers who have only *interpreted* the world—and nothing else. Then, as the second part shows, the Thesis embarks on a thoroughly planned journey in quest of a new activistic philosophy, indispensable for changing the world and of use to it. Admittedly, Marx spoke sharply of philosophy, but not against the contemplative variety as such, if it was a significant example deriving from a great age. His attack was directed against a *particular* type of comtemplative philosophy: that produced by the third-rate Hegelians of his day, which was, rather, a non-philosophy. The toughest of Marx's attacks on these epigones is found (significantly) in his *The German Ideology:* "One must leave philosophy aside, one must emerge from it, and, as an ordinary person, betake oneself to the study of reality, for which there is an enormous amount of material ready to hand, though of course it is unknown to philosophers. If one were then to meet people like Kuhlmann and Stirner again, one would discover

94

CHANGING THE WORLD: MARX'S *THESES ON FEUERBACH*

that one had long since left them 'behind' or below oneself. The same relation exists between philosophy and the study of the real world as between masturbation and sexual love" (MEGA, I, 5, p. 216).

The name of Kuhlmann (a pietistic theologian of the time) and particularly that of Stirner, show clearly that this powerful invective was directed against a particular kind of (non-) philosophy: namely, philosophical gas. It was never directed against Hegel's philosophy or other great philosophies of the past, no matter how contemplative these may have seemed. Marx would have been the last to fail to recognize in the concrete Hegel (the most erudite encyclopaedist since Aristotle) a "study of the real world." Such a reproach was indeed leveled against Hegel, but by minds vastly different from Marx's and Engels': the ideologists of Prussian reaction, and later "revisionism," and other *"Realpolitiker"*—as is well known. Marx speaks in quite different terms of the real philosophy before him even in *The German Ideology,* where he refers to it as if to show that he was entering creatively upon a real inheritance. In the earlier Introduction to *A Critique of Hegel's Philosophy of Right* (1844), Marx had made it quite clear that philosophy could not be transcended without realizing it, and could not be realized without transcending it. The first part, with the accent on "realization," was for the benefit of the "practical ones": "With justification . . ., the practical political party in Germany demands *the negation of philosophy.* It does not err in making this demand, but in restricting itself to a demand which it neither does nor indeed can realize. It believes that it can accomplish this negation by turning its back on philosophy, averting its head and murmuring some wretched and banal phrases. Its limited range of vision does not take in philosophy as a part of *German* reality, or even puts it below the level of German practical life and the theories that serve it. You demand initial adherence to *real* germs of life, but you forget that the real germ of life of the German people has only sprouted inside its cranium up to now. In short: You cannot transcend philosophy without realizing it." The second part, with the emphasis on *transcending,* was intended for the "theoreticians": "The same error, but with factors *reversed,* was committed by the *theoretical* political party, which originated in philosophy. It saw in the present struggle *only the critical struggle of philosophy against the German world,* but failed to realize that *the philosophy of the past* itself belongs to this world and is its complement, albeit an ideal one. Although critical with regard to its counterpart, it was not self-critical in that it started from the *presuppositions* of philosophy and either stopped at philosophy's conclusions, or presented as direct demands and results of philosophy demands and results actually derived from other sources. It did this even though such demands and results—assuming them to be legitimate—could be obtained only by *the negation of previous philosophy,* of philosophy as philosophy. We propose to give a more thorough account of this party [this was done in *The Holy Family* and *The German Ideology,* with the heaviest criticism of the contemplation involved, of the critical "serenity of knowing"]. Its basic defect may be summarized thus: *it believed that it could realize philosophy without transcending it"* (MEGA, I, 1/1, p. 613).

Consequently, Marx offers both parties of the day an antidote for their behavior—the inverted *medicina mentis* required by the situation. He prescribes for the activists a greater degree of realization of philosophy, and for the theoreticians a greater degree of transcension of philosophy. Yet even the "negation" of philosophy (itself so extremely philosophical a concept, and one deriving from Hegel) relates explicitly in the context to *"previous philosophy"* and not to every possible and future manifestation thereof. The "negation" relates to philosophy with truth for its own sake (that is, it is critical of the type which is autarchically contemplative and which interprets the world simply from an antiquarian point of view), but not to the type which is transforming the world in a revolutionary manner. Indeed, within *"previous philosophy"* (which of course is so very different from the pseudo-Hegelians) there exists—notwithstanding all the con-

96

templation—so much "study of the real world," that even German classical philosophy could figure, and with no great stretch of the imagination, among "the three sources and three component parts of Marxism."

What is unmistakably new in the Marxist philosophy consists in the radical transformation of its basis, in its proletarian revolutionary mandate; yet this definitely new element does not demand that the only philosophy capable of producing a concrete transformation of the world should cease to be philosophy—precisely because in the Marxist formulation, philosophy was more philosophy than ever before. For that reason, the triumph of knowledge is celebrated in the second half of Thesis 11, in regard to the *transformation* of the world. Marxism would constitute no change in the true sense of the word were it not antecedently and essentially the theoretical and practical foundation of *true philosophy*—of the philosophy which, with vital power and an application of the cultural heritage, would engage in comprehension of those aspects of reality which bear the seeds of the future within them. Of course, even without any concept, it is often possible to effect change in a spurious sense. Thus the Huns certainly produced change, as did the madness of the Caesars, anarchism, and even the psychopathy of the drivel which Hegel termed "a complete representation of chaos." But *solid* change, notably that leading in the direction of *the realm of freedom,* takes place only on the basis of solid knowledge, and with an increasingly exact mastery of necessity. Since then, it has been philosophers who have consistently transformed the world in this fashion, namely, Marx, Engels, and Lenin. On the other hand, the naïve mechanics of practice and the schematizers laden with quotations have not transformed the world—not even those empiricists whom Engels termed "inductive asses." Philosophical transformation of the world is equipped with unfailing knowledge of the total context of relations, for even if philosophy is not a science superordinate to the other sciences, it still constitutes the unique cognition and conscience of the totality in all the sciences. It is the progressive

97

consciousness of the advancing totality, seeing that the latter does not itself exist as a fact, but is to be seen only in the gigantic interaction of becoming with what has not yet come to be. Philosophical transformation is, therefore, one unfolding according to the dimension of the situation as analyzed, the dialectical trend, objective laws, and real possibility.

For this reason, philosophical transformation ultimately takes place on the horizon of a future which can be known on the basis of a Marxist approach but not on the basis of any contemplative, interpretative standpoint. From this vantage point, Marx also succeeded in rising above the two aforementioned antithetical positions relating to the fulfillment or the transcension of philosophy (the former emphasized against the standpoint of the "activists," the latter against the "theoreticians"). The *dialectical unity* of these respective emphases, when correctly understood, is expressed at the end of the Introduction: "Philosophy can be realized only by the transcending of the proletariat, and the proletariat can be transcended only by realizing philosophy." Now the abolition-by-raising-up of the proletariat, when understood not only as a class, but also as the most obvious human symptom of self-alienation, is undoubtedly a long process; indeed, a full sublation in this sense coincides with the last act of communism and with the intention expressed by Marx in the *Economic and Philosophic Manuscripts*—that is, a perspective oriented to the most extreme philosophical *"eschaton":* "Only here will man's *natural* existence be his *human* existence, and will nature have become human for him. Therefore, *society* is the fulfillment of the essential unity of man and nature, the true resurrection of nature, the thoroughly executed naturalism of man and the thoroughly executed humanism of nature" (MEGA, I, 3, p. 152). Here the ultimate perspective of world transformation as sought by Marx shines forth. Its fundamental idea, the knowledge-and-conscience basic to all praxis, in which the still distant totality is reflected, undoubtedly demands as much innovation in philosophy as it produces a resurrection of nature.

The Point of Archimedes:
Knowledge Oriented Not Only to What Is Past
but Essentially to What Is Yet to Come

For the first time, man's mind had become this powerful; finally, it came to understand its own potentiality. This was possible precisely because man had abandoned his former being, which he frequently elevated to a false position; and because he had become a truly political melody, finally tearing himself away from what was past and from mere contemplation, and thus emerging into the present. Moreover, man emerged into the present at a time which refused to regard mind as ethereal but on the contrary used it as a material force. To understand all this it is necessary to note the point of time at which, together with the other early writings of Marx, the *Theses on Feuerbach* entered into this powerful light. Marx wrote about this in the *Communist Manifesto* somewhat later, in 1848: "The Communists turn their attention chiefly to Germany, because that country is on the eve of a bourgeois revolution that is bound to be carried out under more advanced conditions of European civilization, and with a much more developed proletariat than that of England was in the seventeenth, and of France in the eighteenth century, and because the bourgeois revolution in Germany will be but the prelude to an immediately following proletarian revolution." This, therefore, was the source of the particular impetus (not felt by Feuerbach) which brought the new philosophy, *in statu nascendi*, upon the barricades. Thesis 4 had already revealed the point of Archimedes from which the old world is to be lifted out of its hinges and a new one installed—in the contemporary "secular basis": "Therefore, the latter first must be understood in its contradiction and then revolutionized in practice by the elimination of the contradiction" (version edited by Engels). What, ultimately, had the incipient philosophy of the revolution discovered, the starting point of the Eleven Theses? Surely it was not the new proletarian mandate alone, no matter how decisively it had torn itself away from mere contempla-

99

tion, and was determined not to accept things as they were, or indeed permit them to continue indefinitely. And it was not only the critical and creative acquisition and application of German philosophy, British political economy, and French socialism—no matter how necessary these three ferments (especially Hegel's dialectics and Feuerbach's renewed materialism) were for the development of Marxism. The ultimate achievement which finally led to the point of Archimedes, and hence to the new conception of theory and praxis, was something which had not occurred in any previous philosophy, and indeed was not yet fully apparent in Marx himself. "In bourgeois society . . .," said the *Communist Manifesto,* "the past dominates the present; in communist society, the present dominates the past." The present dominates, *together with the horizon it contains,* which is the horizon of the future, that provides the fiux of the present with its specific space—the space and scope of a new and practicable better present. Therefore, the incipient philosophy of the revolution, that is, its transformability in the direction of the Good, opens ultimately at and in *the horizon of the future;* with the knowledge of the New, and with power to take the way to it.

Until then, however, all knowledge had been essentially oriented to the past, seeing that only the latter is available for consideration. Consequently, the new remained completely out of conceptual range, and the present in which the emergent new had its front line remained an embarrassment. This old traditional powerlessness was increased particularly by commodity thought. For, the transformation under capitalism of all men and things into commodities not only alienated them, but brought the realization that the thought pattern of commodities is in fact only the "up-dated" thought pattern of givenness and facticity. Because of this "facticity," it was particularly easy to forget what had not yet become a fact and was still in the process of becoming [*fieri*]; even as it was possible to forget the producer because of the reified product, and to forget the open future lying ahead of mankind because of the apparently fixed and completed region behind him.

100

Yet the erroneous mutual relationship of knowledge and the past is very much older, and has its origin at a point where the function of work in cognition was not considered in epistemology, with the result that knowledge was identified with sight, and the object of knowledge became something already entirely formed, and essentiality having-beenness pure and simple. This is the realm of Platonic *anamnesis:* "For," says Socrates in the dialogue *Meno* (81b-82a), alluding to vision in the *primal past* of the soul, "seeking and learning are actually nothing but recollection."

Such is the power of this antique contemplative theory— notwithstanding all the social changes in the concept of knowledge—that it kept philosophy until Marx not only in a contemplative miasma, but fixed *in a relationship to what was past*—a relationship built into all contemplation.

Even for the philosopher of evolution, Aristotle, essence is "what-was-being," in the sense of fixed determinability and formed contours. Even for Hegel, the great dialectical philosopher of process, events are completely weighed down by their accomplished history, and essence is reality that has already become, and thus "one with its manifestation." This same limitation was noted by Marx himself, in respect to Feuerbach: "Feuerbach's whole deduction in respect to the relation of men to one another only goes to prove that men need and *have always needed* one another. He wants to establish consciousness of this fact and, like the other theoreticians, to effect only a correct awareness of an *existing* fact; whereas the particular concern of the real communist is to overthrow the status quo" (*The German Ideology*, p. 31). The effect of all this was that the spirit of *anamnesis* sought its cognitive power at the very point where there was least scope for the *present* (let alone the *future*) as far as decision-making was concerned. The inevitable result was that the mere relationship of knowledge-oriented-to-the-past to questions of the present (let alone to problems of decision regarding the future) was almost like pouring liquid from one container to another; or, from the extremely myopic standpoint of the

101

bourgeoisie (without discarding its traditional class outlook), this relationship was, so to say, comfortable only in the seclusion of the past. The farther back in time objects were, the more adequate their closed form seemed in the eyes of the contemplative "observer"—and hence the more comforting to the bourgeois.

Hence, in regard to this relationship of knowledge and the past, the Crusades, so to speak, permit more "scientific validity" than the last two World Wars, and Egypt, much deeper in the past, offers more than the Middle Ages. Indeed, the apparently total past of physical nature stands (or stood) here as a sort of super-Egypt of Egyptian "potential" far, far back in the past, with the granite having-beenness of a matter which was termed dead—not without methodical satisfaction.

How different all this became in Marxism, and how effective it became—in respect to the present precisely. Its *new and thorough science, oriented to occurrence and change,* maintains itself at the front line of happening, in the actuality of decisions made now, in the controlling of a trend oriented to the future. From the Marxist point of view, even the past is not divided into increasingly antiquarian stages, for history— primally communistic, a history of class struggles—does not make even its most remote epoch into a museum. Even less does history make more recent periods a moratorium remote from science, as happens in bourgeois contemplation. One result is that considerable areas of bourgeois scholarship, having no concrete epistemological relation to the present, are helpless when the present requires a decision from them. Or else (as in most recent times) they sell themselves to anti-Bolshevism, above and beyond every class interest, with scandalous ignorance and folly. Even the quite different scientific pioneers of bourgeois society, who were securely related to the great and pure ideologies of the seventeenth and eighteenth centuries (which were supported by a relationship with present and future) always reacted to the emergence of their own revolutionary class with illusions or high-flying extravagant ideals. The reason was not only the specific class

102

barrier, but the barrier before the future, which until Marx was always posited and fixed by the class barrier. All these factors united, and the longer it took, the more powerful was the union with *anamnesis* or the barrier of contemplative and static knowledge against what was really approaching and coming up. Similarly—but altogether decisively—where *the relationship of knowledge and the past* sees in the present only confusion, and in the future only spray, wind, and formlessness, there *the relationship of knowledge and tendency* apprehends and seizes the where-to and wherefore of its knowledge: as the mediated reconstruction of the world.

Hence Marxism, the dialectical-historical science of the knowledge of *tendency,* is the interposed futuristic science of reality plus the objectively real possibility contained within it, and is wholly concerned with the goal of action. It is impossible to imagine a more illuminating contrast to any theory which is only a restatement *(anamnesis)* of what has already taken place, and its sundry variations. The contrast is as true of the illuminating method of Marxism as the elucidation of the unfinished matter which it illuminates. *Only the horizon of the future, as Marxism brings it into knowledge and relates it to the past as the corridor to the future, gives reality its dimension of reality.*

One must not forget at this point the new locus of the Archimedean point from which the leverage of history will be attempted. This, too, does not lie far behind us in the past, and in the finished product to which earlier materialism, satisfied with mere observation, had reduced the world. The further effect of this kind of reductionism was wholly retrogressive, and particularly so once it had made its contribution to demythizing rationalization. It dissolved historical into biological and these in turn into chemical and physical phenomena, arriving ultimately at an atomic "basis" for everything and everybody. The result was that even a primarily historical phenomenon, such as the Battle of Marathon, was reduced to muscular movements, with the Greeks, the Persians, and the whole historical content of the battle resolved into completely

103

subhistorical reflexes. The latter in turn became physiological processes of an organic chemical nature; and organic chemistry, in its turn, common to all forms of life, finally ended up in the dance of the atoms as the universal "basis" of every thing and every person. By such a procedure not only would the Battle of Marathon (which should have been *explained*) disappear completely, but the entire world that has been built up would have declined into the generality of a universal mechanics, losing all its phenomena and all its subtle variations. Mechanistic materialism views such a reduction of phenomena to their atomic structure as its basic and exclusive concern. By such a procedure we are certainly in the night which Hegel called "the night in which all cows are black." What is lacking is precisely what the first great materialist, Democritus, termed "the rescue of phenomena," and which he set up as the appropriate method of science.

It is at this point that Feuerbach, with his "anthropological," non-physicalistic materialism, rendered a great service to the young Marx—a service recognized throughout the *Theses.* Admittedly, atoms and all biology are the basis of every subsequent development in the process of evolution, yet the "starting point," as Engels later termed it in his *Dialectics of Nature,* and subsequently the Archimedean point for history, is—from the viewpoint of Marxism—the working man. His social methods of satisfying his needs, the "totality of social relationships," set by Marxism in place of the abstract man in Feuerbach's analysis, and the social process of exchange with nature itself: all this is now set up by Marxism as the only relevant and actual basis as far as the realm of history and culture is concerned. Hence Marxism also teaches a material basis, indeed one much more definitely material than that of the invisible atomic processes; but, precisely because it is more definite, and related to the unique development of history, it does not turn historical phenomena and characters into the darkness of night. On the contrary, it sheds a genuine light for the first time, and reveals the Archimedean point, that is, the relationship of man to other men and to nature.

CHANGING THE WORLD: MARX'S *THESES ON FEUERBACH*

Precisely because historical materialism, in contrast to the one-sided variety based only on natural science, was not contemplative, it discovered at the specific location of its Archimedean point not only the key of theory but the lever of practical activity. Hence Marxism was least apt to destroy this lever and, correspondingly, least apt to destroy the higher, new organization of living matter toward which the lever was exerting its leverage.

Let us look once again at Thesis 10: "The standpoint of the older type of materialism is civil society; the standpoint of the new materialism is *human* society or socialized humanity." Moreover, any transformation of the world along these lines will take place only in a world which is *qualitatively transformable,* and alterable in essence, and not in a world of mechanical constancy and of pure quantitativeness, in which history counts for nothing. Even so, there can be no world susceptible to change unless the horizon of the objectively real possibility within it has been grasped; otherwise, even its dialectic would be a sort of cyclical repetition or substitution.

Indeed, in the dialectics of Marxism, which spans the world, a far greater power of creation became evident, and entered into the domain of science. This hope of a real science of life, that it might really become what was implied by this term, became an historical event in Marx. It is not complete, for it is but a unique forward march into the transformable world—which presages happiness. The whole message of the *Theses* is that a humanity which has become socialized, in an alliance with a nature adjusted to it, represents the transformation of the world into a real homeland for man.

MARX AND THE DIALECTICS OF IDEALISM

When the student Marx arrived in Berlin in 1836, Hegel had been dead for five years, but his spirit dominated everyone as though he were still there, looking over their shoulders—even those of his enemies. The young Marx wrote to his father that he had chained himself more and more firmly to Hegel despite the latter's "grotesque craggy melody." Under the influence of the left-Hegelians, then Feuerbach above all, Marx moved from mind to man. He went on from the idea to need and its social machinations, from movements of the intellect to real movements rising out of economic interest. But if Marx set Hegel upon his feet in this manner, the latter also showed that he was at least not unacquainted with the cloven hoof. An unguarded statement by the great idealist is apposite here— one to which not only the young but even the decidedly materialistic Marx would have strongly assented. In 1807 Hegel wrote from Bamberg, where he was eking out a livelihood as an editor, to his friend in Jena, Major Knebel: "Experience has convinced me of the truth of the biblical dictum and I have made it my pole star: think first of meat and raiment, and then the kingdom of God will be added unto you of itself" (*Werke,* XVII, pp. 629 f.). Of course, Matthew (6, 33) says just the reverse. But this quotation constitutes an additional contribution (which can also be verified in the young Marx) to the fruitful insight that the Hegelian idea does not always require too much turning over for it to show a red lining.

Now, this very turning-over process, a primary concern with Hegel, was most appropriate and practicable in regard to the dialectician Hegel himself. For, in his capacity as a dialectician, he had permitted that to happen through the idea which could occur only through bodies and persons, yet he often also permitted only what was happening in concrete existential relations to be reflected in the idea. This general dialectical lawfulness Marx and Engels (as the latter put it in his preface to *Anti-Dühring*) "rescued by transforming it into the materialistic interpretation of Nature and history." For Marx, a concretized dialectics controls all his analyses, and overlays all his hopes, as a breakthrough of the new beyond the enveloping crust, and as a preserving transcendence of whatever may still be so retained. This is what enables Marx, in contrast to the abstract utopians, to see misery not only as misery but as the turning point. This concretized dialectics convinces Marx that the proletariat must not be regarded only as the negation of man, but that—precisely because of the extreme depersonalization suffered by the proletariat—it must be viewed as the precondition for "the negation of negation."

What disappears in Marx is Hegel's interpretation of dialectics as a mere to-and-fro conversation in a cosmic discourse, so to speak, of a world architect with himself; Marx completely abandons this false mental subject of Hegel's. But dialectics as an *actual process,* once the idealistic appearance falls away, becomes truly visible for the first time; it is the law of matter in motion. Another Hegelism dropped by Marx is that of the mind doubly spiritualized as reminiscence which, in the dialectical procession of minds, ultimately eliminates *not* minds but, on the contrary, the course, the process, or—as

107

Marx says—the space of production, which is Time. Yet the real totality and its really universal substrate now become really visible—as *dialectical, processual matter which retains its openness.* This does not reduce the fundamental essence to something past or to some substance which in every aspect has been wholly "ready" from the outset. Therefore, dialectical matter is not by any means the unchangeable type of mechanical materialism. It does not form a block with some dialectically decorative slogan, which scarcely scratches the surface of the block, let alone transform it.

The totality of dialectical matter does not lie at the horizon of the past, as is the case with the remembrance mind of Hegel, and with mechanical matter—as has been true since Democritus, but at the horizon of the future. Dialectical materialism now envisages matter as being dynamically active in the direction of the future, to which the past itself refers. It interprets matter not only as the precondition of all phenomena but as something which has not yet entered into full phenomenal existence: that which not only permits the possibility of being, but exists in possibility.

Marx reproaches Hegel thus: "In Hegel's philosophy of history as in his philosophy of nature, the son gives birth to the mother, mind to nature, the Christian religion to paganism, the result to the beginning." But in mechanistic materialism, the beginning does not give birth even to a result; its matter remains unfruitful, whereas dialectical matter has before it the entire life of the process proclaimed by Hegel. Hence dialectical-materialistic knowledge has dethroned the Hegelian *logos* together with all its ossified restlessness and all its uneasy rigidity, but has appropriated its historical realm. Therefore, a conscious production of history and an active relating of it to a really complete totality (which does not yet exist as such) now arises.

This then is the conversion process between Hegel and Marx: the rectification of the procession of minds as, now, a terrestrial process, and of a fixed content of memory as, now, an inexhaustible quarry of dialectical matter. The logic of the

MARX AND THE DIALECTICS OF IDEALISM

matter provides the explanation why so much of the philosophical terminology of that day (for example, "alienation," "objectification," "transformation of quantity into quality," and so on) continues to survive on the agenda of Marxism. Above all, Hegel's *Phenomenology* and *Logic* have remained most vital in Marxism because of dialectics. But this does not exhaust the heritage, for, actually, works of really systematic Hegelian philosophy contain dialectics in ever new and varied forms. Engels wrote a *Dialectics of Nature,* following the trial of Hegel; and Marx took over from Hegel's *Philosophy of Right* the fundamental distinction between civil society and the State, as well as much more substantive and not purely "methodological" material.

Moreover, Hegel's *Aesthetics* is largely constructed on the basis of social relations and coordinated with them in a way that shows the *concrete* intention as much as it betrays a desire to show their significance in terms of the "ideal." Wherever his ideological treatment extends to culture, Marx always refers to Hegel's ideas about art. Lenin had all these references in mind when he characterized Marx's theory as the direct and immediate *continuation* of the theory of the greatest representatives of philosophy, political economy, and socialism" ("The Sources and Three Component Parts of Marxism"). Hence extensive sections of Hegel's work—not least, in this regard, in the area of the philosophy of religion (left-Hegelians, Feuerbach)—belong to the history of Marxist mediation—which is of course incomplete as yet. Even if it is a continuation, Marxism is and remains an *innovation* with respect not only to Hegel but to all previous philosophy. The reason for this is that in Marxism, unlike the past, philosophy appears not as that of a class society but as one espousing the transcendence of a class society. Yet this innovation was no sudden miracle; on the contrary, without classical German philosophy, without this mediation, it would not exist.

Man, says Marx, differs from the beaver in that he plans his construction. In order to succeed in his activities he must have considered his enterprise in his head first, and developed some

109

ideas about it. But not in the fashion so frequently found in Hegel, that a man carries a concept or a schematic movement of concepts into things from the outside. Knowledge does not come from the depths of one's individual mind or just from contemplation of it. It takes place solely as a reflection of actual events and their relatively enduring modes of being (categories). Yet Marx recognizes facts as such as little as Hegel: to him they are only factors or moments of processes. From this processual character it follows that every knowledge has its own time, and that philosophy—as Hegel says—really "is its time" (and the time immediately ensuing contained therein) "comprehended in thoughts."

Here Marx assimilates Hegel completely, but in a characteristically sharpened form, far distant from mere contemplation: "It is not enough that thought should drive toward reality, for reality must also drive toward thought." The comprehending subject is, in dialectical mutuality, dependent upon the historical maturity or ripeness of the object to be comprehended. In this, the subject as the bearer of merely intellectual contemplation is quite distinct from the subject of real history. In Hegel, both coincided to such a degree that the thought-generating subject was also the history-generating subject, although the contemplative subject, that of philosophy, comes too late. But even this subsequent consciousness of the philosopher, to which Hegel reduces the subject of the thinking, is still basically the history-subject, except that he is *post festum,* and only resting on his laurels. In Hegel's cosmic coin, thinking and being, heads and tails, coincide, even though the "head" has only the status of a pensioner, and so merely *records* the world course—which the "head" supposedly is.

Marx, on the other hand, sees in the thought-generating subject nothing more than a bearer of false consciousness, of contemplation outside of the real, that is, the process of production. Or else, on the other hand, Marx evaluates thought, insofar as it is involved with occurrent reality, as itself a factor in the transformation process; only then does it become (unconditionally) generative of history. As class con-

110

sciousness, as revolutionary science, it becomes a particularly powerful force, exerting an influence, in turn, upon production and the economic base, and it belongs to the history-generating subject, to history engendered by *consciousness.*

For Marx, however, the fundamental subject is never mind but man, economic and social. Nor is this the same abstract man, man as a mere species being, as in Feuerbach, but man as a totality of social relationships, changing through history—and, in the last analysis, a being as yet undiscovered and unemancipated.

Thus the course of the dialectical relationship between subject and object in which one always corrects and changes the other, primarily in and on the socio-economic basis of history, which—to a considerable extent—is the same as the superstructure; it occurs in the social realm of interests, not in the celestial realm of ideas. Marx interprets Hegel's *Phenomenology* especially as if Hegel, despite his own idealism, had espoused such a material dialectics: The "great achievement" of the *Phenomenology* is first "that Hegel conceived the self-production of man as a process"; but secondly, and above all, "that he grasps the nature of *labor,* and comprehends objective man (true, because real man) as the product of his *own labor.*" Therefore, the self-production of absolute knowledge has given way to the self-production of man through work; and the autonomous self-development of spirit (a laborious process even in Hegel—one wonders why) has given way to real history. It exists only in a materially dialectical form, riddled with class struggles, with the "emancipation of man" only at the end—which has not arrived.

Hegel ended his *History of Philosophy* with a variation on a quotation from Virgil's *Aeneid: "Tantae molis erat, se ipsam cognoscere mentem";* "What a burden for the mind to know itself." Marx always interpreted this burden as more than intellectual, even though he, together with Hegel, regarded the inscription at Delphi "Know thyself" as the theme of human history. For all that, he was far removed from any intention of defining self-knowledge (with the left-Hegelians) as the mere

111

"philosophy of self-consciousness." Self-knowledge became non-contemplative and that of the working man, who sees himself in it both as the commodity which he becomes through alienation, and as a value-generating subject who transcends by revolutionary activity the commodity character forced upon him. This is the practical implementation of the Delphic admonition in Marx—the transcendence of alienation by its conversion into praxis. It is this very alienation that drives the process of production and knowledge of the human relations determined by it as far as possible into providence, into a reified and unintelligible destiny.

Hence dialectics must learn not to remain a procedure executed upon things. Not even Hegel intended it thus, for he disapproved of any methodology separated from matter; it was not thus even in the circumambient theory of knowledge. Nevertheless, Hegel developed his dialectics as a purely idealistic one which, insofar as it dealt with a nation and people, always did so, however, according to the standard of a logical *a priori*.

For Marx, on the other hand, dialectics is never a method according to which he reworks history, but is identical with history itself. The quasi-bourgeoisie within feudal society, the proletariat within bourgeois society, the crises arising out of the faulty relationship between the already collective modes of production in large-scale industry and private capitalist productive relations: all these contradictions engendered in contemporary society were not methodologically introduced into the matter, and were not superficial manifestations which could be easily put right. They belong, as Marx taught, to the dialectics of its essence. It is the contradiction with society developed to an extreme form that is really moving toward its own dissolution—not something in a book dealing with reality where satisfaction is afforded to the mind, but everything remains as it was in the country visited. That the old remains unchanged nowhere, that instead, by virtue of the productive force of revolutionary dialectical knowledge, it may be possible to arrive at something new and better: this is made possible by the real dialectics of the matter itself. It is made possible by a material condition in which no stone will remain unturned, in which indeed through man knowing and acting, the ultimate form of matter, it will be possible to build a house and home with the movable stones—in short, what the old utopians termed *regnum hominis,* a world for men.

In order to move the world forward in this direction, with man as a part of the world and in the world, it must be what it is for Marx—a material process. All the categories and the various spheres (law, art, science) function solely within a reality which is revolutionized in history. They are modes of existence which do not form an ever-constant, closed system, but, on the contrary, vary from one society to another. These "spheres" (law, art, science) never enjoy an autonomous life or autarchy—as in Hegel.

In regard to Nature as well, Marx posits a uniform historical medium (mediative essence): "We know only one science, the science of history. History may be considered from two aspects and may be divided into the history of Nature and the history of man. Nevertheless, the two cannot be sundered; as long as men exist, the history of Nature and the history of men exist in a reciprocally determinative relationship" *(The German Ideology).*

In all this, the main point is ever and again that the Hegelian dialectics, having been set right way up, is not to remain contemplative. The subject in the subject-object relation of universal historical materialism is defined as dynamically active, as really productive.

Everywhere in Marx's works, this anti-contemplation motif is directed against materialism of the older type, as against Hegel. In his doctoral dissertation on Democritus, Marx had noted that Democritus had omitted the "energizing principle." Quite consistently, therefore, he had reproached Feuerbach for teaching a materialism that was only contemplative, far too objectivistic. In Feuerbach, much more so than in Hegel, reality was "conceived" only in the form of *objects,* or as *observation,* but not as *sensuous human activity,* praxis, not subjectively" *(Theses on Feuerbach).* Hence, certainly in Hegel, "in contradistinction to materialism, the *active* aspect of reality was developed abstractly by idealism, which, of course, does not recognize real sensuous activity as such." Ultimately, Marx held that the "subjective" or "intensive" element was by no means completely absent from Hegel, as the anti-Hegelians Kierkegaard and Schelling had surmised from the vantage point of their "positive" idealism. Marx emphasized the presence of the *subject-*object relationship of Hegel's dialectics in regard to the labor process; and he asserted that the subject, so very abstract in Hegel, was not absent, being a material force. Marx taught that human life existed solely within the totality of determinative social relationships, but he also taught that man, by virtue of his labor, was the producer and transformer of these relationships. Instead of the mechanistic cosmic bustle in which, apart from external necessity, there is no meaning at all, Marx kept alive an historical evolutionary humanism which derived from Leibniz, and which was mediated to him through Hegel. In this humanism, the whole world is an open system of enlightenment developing dialectically. Its focal point is humanity, objectively alienated, and among things which are no longer alienated.

This, then, is the life of Hegel in Marx. A new type of society—not the one decaying *spiritually* in the post-Hegel period—claimed the heritage of German classical philosophy.

Proof:

Philosophers have only *interpreted* the world in different ways; the point is to *change* it.

Theses on Feuerbach

The Old Hegelians had comprehended everything once it was reduced to some Hegelian logical category. The Young Hegelians

114

criticized everything in that they introduced religious notions or explained it as theology. The Young Hegelians and the Old Hegelians are united in their belief in the dominion of religion, of concepts, and of universality in the existing world. Only, one group attacks this domination as usurpation, while the other celebrates it as legitimate.

Once the dominant ideas are separated from the dominant individuals and, above all, from the relationships that result from a given stage of productive relations, and thus the conclusion is reached that ideas are always dominant in history, it is very easy to extract from these various ideas *the* idea, the notion, and so on, as dominant in history, and hence to interpret all these individual ideas and concepts as "self-determination" of *the* concept developing in history . . . This is what speculative philosophy has done.

The German Ideology
(MEGA, I, 5, pp. 9, 37 f.)

Does critical criticism believe that it has even made a start in the knowledge of historical reality as long as it omits from the movement of history the theoretical and practical behavior of man toward Nature, together with natural science and industry? Or does it imagine that it has actually already come to know any period of history unless it has come to know, for example, the industry of that period, the direct mode of production of life itself? Yet all that spiritualistic and theological critical criticism knows of history—at least so it fancies—are the political, literary, and theological actions of rulers and States. Just as it separates thought from the senses, the soul from the body, and itself from the world, so it separates history from natural science and industry and locates the birthplace of history not in coarse material production on earth but in the misty cloud formation in the heavens.

The Holy Family (1844-45)
(MEGA, I, 3, p. 327)

Hegel is guilty of a double inadequacy: first, he expounds philosophy as the existence of Absolute Spirit, yet refuses to explain the actual philosophical individual as Absolute Spirit: secondly, he allows Absolute Spirit to make history as Absolute Spirit only *in appearance.*

115

Since Absolute Spirit becomes conscious as the creative world spirit only in the philosopher, *post festum,* its making of history exists only in consciousness, in the opinion and mind of the philosopher, only in the speculative imagination.

The Holy Family
(MEGA, I, 3, p. 258)

The great achievement of Hegel's *Phenomenology* and its final result, the dialectics of negativity as the moving and productive principle, is first that Hegel conceives the self-production of man as a process, objectification as loss of the object, as alienation and transcendence of this alienation; and, therefore, that he grasps the nature of *labor,* and comprehends objective man (true, because real man) as the product of his *own labor.*

Economic and Philosophic Manuscripts of 1844
(MEGA, I, 3, p. 156)

I openly declared myself to be a disciple of that great thinker, and here and there in *Capital,* when examining the theory of value, I even flirted with his characteristic modes of expression. The mystification which the dialectic suffered in Hegel's hands did not in the least prevent him from being the first to set forth its general forms of operation in a comprehensive and conscious fashion. With him, however, it is standing on its head. It must be turned right side up again in order to discover the rational kernel within the mystical shell. In its mystified form, the dialectic became the German method, as it appeared to glorify the existing order. In its rational form, it is a scandal and an abomination to the bourgeoisie and its doctrinaire spokesmen, because it includes in its positive understanding of the existing state of things, at the same time, recognition of the negation of that state, of its necessary disappearance; because it observes every historically developed form in the flow of movement, and thus in its transient aspect as well; and because it lets nothing delude it, and is essentially critical and revolutionary.

Capital
(Preface to the second edition, 1873)

116

MARX AND THE DIALECTICS OF IDEALISM

The same spirit builds philosophical systems in the brain of philosophers that builds railroads with the hands of working men. Philosophy does not stand apart from the world, any more than the brain exists outside man because it is not in the stomach. Yet philosophy, of course, exists in the world with the brain before it stands with its feet upon the ground, whereas many other spheres of human life have been rooted in the earth and have plucked the fruit of the world long before they suspect that the brain is also of this world or that this world is the world of the brain.

Rheinische Zeitung
(July 14, 1842)

Just as philosophy finds its material weapons in the proletariat, so the proletariat finds its intellectual weapons in philosophy. As soon as the lightning of thought has thoroughly penetrated this naïve soil of the people, the Germans will be emancipated to become men . . . Philosophy cannot be realized without the transcendence of the proletariat; the proletariat cannot be transcended without the realization of philosophy.

Introduction to *A Critique*
of Hegel's Philosophy of Right (1844)

THE UNIVERSITY, MARXISM,
AND PHILOSOPHY

In our case the mutual task requiring mutual trust is learning:
the acquisition and increase of knowledge. It is the labor
involved in obtaining illumination, the procurement of resources for seeing and comprehending, in order to proceed and
act correctly.

As the subject of my inaugural lecture I have choosen "The
University, Marxism, and Philosophy." These are three great
categories. The opponents but also the doubters of the new
world which has arisen and is going to grow more sturdy have
established a grotesque distinction between these three categories. According to Jaspers, the university, as the locus of
free investigation, must take a rather reluctant attitude to
Marxism, as much because of the *freedom* of research as of
research itself, that is, *its scientific nature.* Among the reactionaries of America, Marx, the emancipator of the weary and
the heavy-laden, is regarded as a near-criminal—an opinion
which not even the German reactionaries would share. It will
be recalled that bourgeois political economy, even before
the Weimar Republic, recognized Marx, *nolens volens,* as the

118

greatest theoretician after its own Adam Smith. Yet for the most part, among the partisan ideological friends of ostensibly unbiased academic research, Marx very likely passes as something that cannot readily be squared with such research. For the most part he seems to them a mixture of theory and propaganda, hardly to be associated with so-called "truth for its own sake." In this connection the American reactionaries, notwithstanding all other differences, have at least this in common with their German counterparts: that they maintain their substantial ignorance of the object of their hate. Hence all kinds of self-fabricated chimeras are passed off as the materialistic philosophy of history—this in order to frighten the sheep. For sheep are always amazed and are downright pained when sometimes it dawns upon them that Marxism can and indeed must be studied just as objectively as, for example, thermodynamics. Instead, one generally encounters a kind of circuitous avoidance, which is reminiscent to some extent of the annihilation of Einstein by Nazi physics. But this is surely neither free research nor the scientific attitude. Wanton reaction suppresses the connection between Marx and classical economics which he, as the greatest investigator of economic phenomena, inherited and transcended in a new stage. Moreover, such reaction suppresses the close connection between Marx and Engels and German philosophy, the dialectics of which, as is well known, Marx brought to concrete fulfillment, rectified, and set right way up. Marx and Engels held upright and unforgotten Hegel, his *Phenomenology of the Spirit,* his *Logic,* his *Philosophy of History,* and *Aesthetics,* and even his *Natural Philosophy,* at a time when the bourgeois neo-Kantians and other epigones were making sport of Hegel or speaking of him as though he were a dead dog. Moreover, this was happening in the German universities, and at a time when the light of classical German philosophy and of a *new one* was burning only in Marxism.

Admittedly, there are exceptions. There have been borrowings and there has been an improvement in the judgment, if not in the will. Since the aforementioned mockery of Hegel (which

119

continues in so-called positivism), it has been noised abroad that without him and, indeed, without Marx, even if he is not specifically named, it would be impossible for positivism to maintain its scientific pursuit in tact. A so-called neo-Hegelianism has come into being: but this is only a sterile and indeed reactionary formation, a sort of review course from Kant to Fichte to Hegel. In this process, Hegel is dated back to Fichte, indeed to the darkest areas of Romanticism. Hegel is so thoroughly separated from the conclusions which he reached beyond Feuerbach and in the direction of Marx, that he is also rendered immune to the *progress* of science and truth.

On the other hand, outside philosophy there developed a bourgeois *sociology,* whose older representatives, such as Spencer and Comte, could not have theorized as they did without Hegel, nor have survived, no matter how shallow their intrepretations of him were. Similarly, most of the newer endeavors of this sort have lived, or continue to live, off a concealed, suppressed, or denatured Marx. Particularly the sociology of knowledge, inaugurated by Scheler and Karl Mannheim, wholly imitates the Marxist analysis of ideology, but in a counterfeit form. Such doctrine sounds like jazz without the beat, and yet universities have permitted themselves to be diverted from the primary concern by such derivations. At universities everywhere the sedulous bourgeois apes of Marxism are at work. Now that their own class no longer provides correct understanding, they find themselves forced to use against Marxism certain purloined and transformed Marxist concepts. One example is the relationship between ideology and classes: on this basis Marxism itself then seems to be relativized in Frankfurt, London, and Chicago, as though it were a matter of class and not, indeed, the way to a classless society.

It no longer does to controvert Marx from the standpoint of a reserve officer and to remove Marxism from the university. Therefore, Marxism as the truth must be overcome by corruption, by fatal evasions, by concealments, by complete neglect, and by forged signatures. Yet all this takes place on the pretext

120

that the university and Marxism, or free philosophy and Marxism, could not exist in any kind of open, unforced relationship. The heaviest propaganda of capitalist interests thus purports to be free research and not propaganda. Actually, however, it becomes clearer from day to day that the students of the humanities in the West are no longer able or permitted to experience the true and the real. While the awareness of truth, the breakthrough of mature reality, is artificially hindered by the reactionaries, this very reaction passes off as freedom the force it uses to circumvent the thing that matters, and represents capitalist apologetics as research undertaken in the service of truth.

Instead of that, it is the task of philosophy to demonstrate and maintain that freedom in the upright and true sense is present only where no mandate of the profit interest exists to corrupt either consciously or unconsciously. Scientific *research* exists only where reason is not prevented from standing at the summit of its time and addressing itself concretely to the present and to the tendencies in reality that are pressing forward toward the future.

Fellow students, we are all united in the conviction that we shall no longer voluntarily remain blind. We desire dynamically to comprehend the time in which we live, to be open toward it and its unique movement, and to share responsibility for keeping its motion unimpeded. Youth cannot, by definition, be the eternal yesterday; and it cannot go forward with its head bowed—an unnatural condition. Furthermore, youth, if it does not disqualify itself and engage in self-deception, can be especially close to the contemporary moment—the turning point —and can have confidence in it. This holds true also for bourgeois youth, and especially for its academic representatives, for it is capable of surveying the horizon of the future, of examining with a penetrating eye, and of learning to discard prejudices—or should make itself capable of so doing. Enlightenment, said Kant, is the emergence of man from self-incurred minority. Indeed, the condition of alienation in which all men and things have become commodities, resulting from capital-

121

ism, has affected not only the *proletariat,* but in like measure the *bourgeoisie,* even if in a more tolerable form. But even to the bourgeoisie, this condition now no longer appears psychologically and spiritually profitable. Hence bourgeois academic youth, too, may and must be interested in comprehending and removing the real causes of the cultural aridity brought about by the modern bourgeoisie—skepticism, relativism, nihilism, and disoriented instability.

To this must be added another distinctive affinity for the good, for the emergent better. The young person as such is someone in whom something is still in the process of emerging—something that has not yet been formed but is germinating and fermenting. This something of which he is not yet conscious, and which is not yet clearly known, and not yet developed unites youth with the *time of crisis* in which we find ourselves. Moreover, the age which contains us is youthful. Insofar as we are permitted to live, insofar as we create for ourselves a place to live in, it is a pleasure to be living in this age, at a time of transformation for which future generations will envy us. The ferment, the storm and stress, unites youth with new creation and productivity; and distinguishes it from all stagnancy. Youth is or can be a period of dawning, and so is not unrelated to the present time in which something new and better is in the process of birth, a difficult birth. Working-class youth, of course, does not need such pointers to organic freshness and openness. It knows, anyhow, that the socio-economic movement is allied with it; its class consciousness works within the current of the time. But even middle-class youth, which has in so many ways been proletarianized by the war, and which has no self-evident common interest with the profit economy of a few families or with the bomber squadrons of capitalism—this section of youth is no longer able to discover and recognize the possibilities inherent in being young, in that which has already died. This is true to the degree which they pursue discovery and knowledge at all, to the degree to which they really want to belong to the future, and not to armed stagnation, with war in mind and certain defeat in the offing.

Therefore, it is wholly advisable to get to know the trends of our age, as derived from the philosophy of history, to act in accordance with them, and so to become worthy of them. Before us lies an open way, leading to a better life; it is ready and clear as never before in history. The skepticisms, relativisms, and nihilisms of a dying society, which began as early as 1919 and hindered or blocked so much knowledge of what was right, have come to an end here; if the West pursues such paths any farther, then may the dead bury their dead. Here in our country there is being established a light that surmounts sleep and tears one out of it; here not every one will turn like a sleeper to his own personal world, but rather—according to the true word of Heraclitus—the world of the waking is common. The alleged freedom of wanting not to know, of brutish obstinacy, of evil intellectual volition, but also of individual humbug and of the kind of unlimited twaddle that goes with it—all this has become completely senseless. Both subjectively and objectively, such pretended freedom is the opposite of real freedom, which always represents a countermove against some external, traditional, unmediated necessity, and on the other hand an alliance with the internal, comprehended, mediated, and controlled necessity of the cause—the actuality that matters. Mere illusory freedom does not engage in a countermove against something imposed upon people and inadequate for them; it is much more inclined to stand in a freely chosen or coerced slavery, like that imposed by capital.

Academic freedom, in particular, is wholly different from ignorant obstinacy and exploited blindness. Indeed, Marxism especially stresses the real freedom of research that generally and without any limitations goes all the way, and which is radical in that it grasps the matter at its *radix,* its root. This sort of research is oriented to realities, and neither remains stuck in mere ideologies nor abdicates before illusions.

Fellow students, a sea of limited possibilities lies before us;

123

what is needed is a learning confidence in those who know the nautical chart, in order increasingly to take advantage of this knowledge. The most appropriate means to this end are furnished by economics and philosophy, that is, dialectical-materialistic philosophy. To teach the latter and to advance it at this local university of a new mid-point is my function. It is the goal of this philosophy to penetrate ever wider and deeper domains of being; it is its task to take over the whole heritage of culture and, in contrast to historicism, actively to maintain it in life. It is its claim and postulate to be able to verify the dictum: whoever is seeking for *truth* must enter the realm opened up by Marx. There is no further truth, there is *no other.*

Youth, I have said, is moving in this direction to the degree to which it regards itself as the bearer of the good which is yet to come. So too morality is moving in this direction as a reluctance any longer to suffer, bear, or affirm the injustice of previous class society. It is socialism that finally takes seriously that goal to which hitherto so many moral teachers worthy of reverence have summoned mankind. Seen from this point of view, the classless society is actually that which has so long been sought for (but in vain) under the name of morality. It was sought for in vain primarily because of a merely private attraction and because of a morality concerned only with individual action; another cause was the circumstance that in our class-stratified and hence antagonistic society the so-called maxims of the will are generally unable to be a so-called principle of general legislation. Hence morality can exist only in unity with *socialist theory,* and also with that type of radical research which leads directly to Marxism, in both its developed and as yet undeveloped areas, and which remains connected with it. Marxism retains this sort of will for the coming good not as a private possession, not in the individual's subjective complex of wishes, and not in any abstract opposition of some abstract ethical pattern to the world. No, this will as taught and directed by Marxism is not private but collective; and it comes to complete expression not in any individual subjective desire for a better type of knowing but, on the

124

contrary, proves itself in an objective superior knowledge in harmony with the real trends of the objective world. In this regard reason can never think highly enough of nor strongly enough about itself; not highly enough, seeing that it entrusts to itself the *key* for opening up reality; not strongly enough, in that it maintains itself steadfastly as a force for change instead of remaining contemplative; in short, it assumes the role of a *leverage* for *changing* the world. This dynamic capacity for praxis is also logically the final proof of a realistically scientific judgment. Precisely as *science,* therefore, Marxism shows the way to concrete action, and does so *not* in spite of the fact that it is a science but *because* it is one; because it represents and itself comprehends the enterprise of science as one of the supreme *productive forces.*

But what belongs in the university and to philosophy if not truth which stands the test? The university is an institution where the entire content of contemporary knowledge is presented in regular rotation. It is arranged in faculties, with economics as the necessary foundation, and with philosophy as the necessary orientation connecting the humanities and the natural sciences. Schelling once gave a course of lectures entitled *On the Method of Academic Study;* by discussing the courses of study in philosophy, medicine, law, and theology, he thought he was able to produce an adequate schema or guide to the decisive areas of the world view of his time. The plan is sublime and completely in the spirit of the *universitas literarum;* and, insofar as there is a will toward universality, and insofar as this is possible, it entails no controversy among the faculties. Our Marxist orientation would obviously draw up the plan quite differently, yet it is precisely the Marxist orientation that is and will remain associated with the university in a unity of theory and practice and of practice and theory that must always be confirmed anew. There is no longer any praxis without the total view called philosophy. And there is no longer any philosophy without an orientation to praxis, that is, to the production of a classless society: the elimination of human alienation and reification. Wherever conscience has

125

knowledge and knowledge conscience, there is no philosophy, and certainly no fulfillment of philosophy, without a struggle against alienation. Revolution is not only the overturning of something existing and false, but signifies in this overturning that man in history is finally moving forward, and makes it possible.

In this connection Marxism has revealed three fundamental doctrines which have to become the essential principles of serious study, particularly in the humanities, but also in the natural sciences, so that the latter are equally wary of any intrusion of ideology—as wary as the more anthropological branches. Such adulteration is more difficult to detect and more difficult to eliminate than the so-called personal equation in astronomy or the static belief in harmony within physics.

The first basic doctrine is that of *surplus* values, squeezed out of the worker. This is the instrumentality whereby every society was based on profit and indeed, *mutatis mutandis,* every class society has maintained itself, together with the division of labor, ideology, and all that goes with it. Ricardo has demonstrated that the value of commodities is determined by the work time required for their production. But if the worker in selling his commodity of labor receives its equivalent value in the form of a wage, the genesis of surplus value for the capitalist remains a riddle, one which from the viewpoint of the bourgeoisie has no possible solution. Marx, however, demonstrated that the worker is not paid the full value of his labor, but only the amount he needs in order to reproduce his power to work. That is, the worker is selling not his work but his power to work. In the unpaid portion of the work, Marx discovered the source of surplus value, and ultimately the basic motivation for the existence and maintenance of the whole commodity-producing society. Marx's work surveyed for the first time the transformation of men and things by capitalist society into commodities, and the ghostlike reduction of all use values by their transformation into exchange values, and thus explained them as phenomena that could be eliminated. Since then, we have known what commodities, the circulation of commodities, and the entire process of the reification of life connected with it really are: a relationship between *men* concealed under a crust of *things,* and of a transitory nature. This insight into the nature of commodities revealed the causation of the increasing pallidity, misery, and vapidity of human life.

The second, and closely related, fundamental doctrine is the *economic,* or the *economic-dialectical interpretation of history.* As is well known, it explains history as the scene of class struggles produced by the development of productive forces and the ever-renewed contradiction between such forces and the traditional relationships of production and forms of society which have become impediments. For a long time, these forms were adequate and beneficial for the modes of production and exchange from which they had been derived in specific cases. With the development of the productive forces, however, frequently at a very early date, cracks appear in the masonry; finally the old form becomes completely untenable, so that what had been reason becomes nonsense, what had been been kindness becomes torment, and what had been a garment becomes a straightjacket and a shackle. Thus the bourgeois entrepreneur, this once progressive force, grew out of the limitations of the guilds and the early markets, and—in 1789—burst through them. Today we live with a contradiction between the productive forces, which, in the major modern industrial sector, have become largely centralized: this makes them and their forms of ownership—which are still dominated by private economic considerations—ripe for social control. This contradiction was eliminated in Russia in 1917, despite the then fierce interventionary wars of capital—and even those of today, which are not exactly restrained. In capitalist countries this contradiction produced ever-deepening crises, which were artificially arrested only by a war economy, together with the whole complex of social sickness and quackery, public uncertainty and fascist deception. But even this actuality is only a portion of that universal historical context which Marx discovered by means of the materialistic philosophy of history,

127

the famous connection of basis and superstructure. In this relationship, social existence determines the ideological consciousness, so that the particular economic and technological relationships always form the basis of the particular societies and their cultural life, whereas politics, law, art, religion, science, and philosophy are comprised in the superstructure, and depend for their form and contents on the social mandate of the class in power at the time. Consequently, there is nothing in the superstructure which is not present in the infrastructure, nor is there anything in the latter which is not mirrored and repeated—though transformed—in the superstructure. Hence the latter is the site of *ideology,* filled with more or less false consciousness regarding the true motivations of the time, that is, the economic and social motives. Often, indeed, as finally became clear under fascism, the superstructure is even filled with conscious deception, with calculated mystification. But in the great ages, that is, in periods when thinkers and artists are really able to stand at the summit of a great age, the superstructure is the location of culture—of a culture which is not in the least devaluated, but transmits its substance and inheritance to us when everything transitory in it, that is, everything that is merely attached to the ideology of the time, is comprehended and dissolved.

Dear fellow students, much nonsense has been spoken concerning the materialistic interpretation of history; it has been accused of abandoning everything except the so-called lowest material interests, and of having no sense of higher things. Unfortunately, vulgar Marxism has itself contributed to this nonsense, as for example in the scandalous statement of the now defunct Kautsky, that the reformation was "nothing other than" the ideological expression of profound changes in the European wool market. But a vulgarized Marxism is not Marxism, and Kautsky's miserable "nothing other than," is particularly incompatible with the true scientific Marxism which everywhere recognizes mutual interactions and influences, and widely ramified intermediate links between superstructure and basis.

128

The time for such unmasking or, rather, denunciation has gone: now the keenness and profundity of Marxism simply will not permit such platitudes. The Marxist criticism of bourgeois culture is something altogether different to economism and sociologism—which are merely second-rate theorizing. So don't allow yourselves to be taken in by reactionary and sentimental hearsay—and this goes, too, for the hearsay deriving from vulgar Marxism and vulgarized materialism— regarding the real status and value of the dialectical, materialistic philosophy of history. Through it scales really fall from the eyes; it causes the ideological formations of the past to topple and pass away—but only when they *deserve* this fate. Through it, on the other hand, the unfulfilled, the elements which have continuing relevance to our circumstances, the elements which may counsel and illuminate—their enduring force *(vis perennis)* stands out as even truer than before. The materialistic philosophy of history is a lamp that dispels the mists, and actually makes it possible to understand the great movements of the past better than they understood or could understand themselves. From the plaster figure and the sanctified mustiness into which the work of our ancestors was so often falsely converted, true authentic value emerges for the first time—through a process of demystification. The holy and purifying water in the depths of all great works is released.

As far as the works of science and philosophy in particular are concerned, the economic interpretation of history frees them of the pseudo-problems of *mere* ideology. This brings about a lightening of the burden; it does not cause impoverishment, but affords enrichment. Matters of primary importance are revealed; and there is knowledge of the real motivations and substance of a period, and of the actual contents within the shell. Through insight into the ideological component of an idea it becomes perfectly clear which problems are of continuing effect, or which constitute the fundamental heritage; and what belongs to past history—in short, what is essential or "sociologically relevant." The implications that still concern us, those with substantive content, have nothing to fear,

129

otherwise Marxism would not be the locus of the cultural heritage.

As to the complaint about disenchantment—so frequently made with a certain sanctimoniousness—we must ask if there is really any place in socialist reconstruction for nihilism within the framework of an existence filled with power, enthusiasm, stability, and faith in a better world. Surely it is modern capitalism that produces this emptiness, this freezing homelessness, with brief intoxications and after then a darkness. It is in modern capitalism that we find a prevailing death wish, as in Heidegger, and in Jaspers' metaphysics of disaster. The capitalists do not see any way out before them, and so they drive toward war, or assert a fundamental hopelessness—which is a concomitant of destruction. In 1918 the term was "the decline of the West"; in 1949 the term is "existentialism" (from "existing no more," a *non existere*), or "ontologism" (from "lost existence"), or nihilism. One thing must be clearly understood: this sort of destruction is produced not by the Marxist analysis of history but by the evil magic of the modern bourgeoisie. Hence let the dead bury the dead. For us the dialectical philosophy of history is a vehicle of life: an approach to a really enduring life in history, and to a future unfulfilled in the past. Anyone who has once savored the materialistic critique will ever after be revolted by all ideological twaddle. But for that very reason he will understand better the realities of life, and the treasures which are not consumed by rust and moths.

The third fundamental doctrine of Marxism concerns itself with *the relation between theory and practice.* This is Marx's basic thesis: hitherto the philosophers have only *interpreted* the world in different ways; now it is necessary to *change* the world.

Moreover, the fact that the philosophers have only interpreted and contemplated the world, but have not intervened in it, has socio-economic grounds. For the division of labor and the interests of the wielders of power separate thought from politics—and thus it has remained in the cell of pure thought.

Philosophers were relegated to the ether of so-called pure thought-in-itself, high above the affairs of real life; and they were often filled with contempt for what the bourgeoisie called "the applied sciences."

By contrast, the science of Marxism is of itself, *ab ovo,* in its method and premisses, a direction to concrete action. Here, too, no misunderstandings should be permitted, although they have often been strengthened by vulgarizations of Marxism, as though mental work had far less value than the calloused hand.

It would be equally erroneous to regard Marxism as related to bourgeois American pragmatism, which holds that the truth value of any knowledge is to be measured by its success—which brings profit and common utility—and that any truth apart from this bourgeois type oriented to profitability is impossible and senseless. This may be true in a country where everybody is a salesman, a seller of himself, but surely *this* kind of "theory-practice" is useless for us. The real theory-practice relationship certainly has nothing whatever to do with the shameful pragmatism of the Nazis, except to reject it. "That is right and that is true which serves the interest of the German people"—namely, German monopoly capitalism. This assertion turned the German universities into whores, and German science into a monster—as it did everything else.

To understand Marxist practice and propaganda as well, we must hold fast to the view that something is true not because it is useful, but always because, insofar as, and to the degree that something is true, it is useful. Something false, by virtue of the fact that it does not conform to reality, really cannot bring about any concrete success for an established period of time. The Reichstag fire could not be successful in the long run, nor could all the onslaughts of capitalism help Chiang Kai-shek. Hence social revolution occurs only in the clockwise sense of truth, that is, in the direction of and in harmony with the solar course of true reality and its process.

I repeat the formula with due consideration, in view of the numerous libels and misunderstanding of the theory-practice relationship: something is not true because it is useful; rather,

131

insofar as and to the degree that it is true, it is useful—in the Marxist theory-practice relationship too.

This establishes the status of the theory in our particular case—from the institutional point of view. Here is a university, that is, a place which leads to excellence through learning. Here battles are fought over *truth,* and fought with penetrating investigation and doctrine, not with slogans or the easy simplifications of agitators; and training is provided for concrete practice precisely through such thoroughness. In this effort, theory and practice cannot be sharply opposed, and so thought of in a non-dialectical fashion. There is a permanent relationship of interaction between them. Theory leads to correct action, and then the ensuing action teaches new approaches to situational analysis and to theory. In this process, knowledge wins honor as never before, seeing that its representatives are no ideological *souteneurs* or time-wasters for the leisure hours of the bourgeoisie, nor even abstract dreamers. Instead, they belong to the general staff of the Right—*the* Just which is in process of emerging. Those who have been taught and the scholars and the sciences finally stand together on the front line of the decision process.

One thing more is important here: as the idealism of pure *theory* comes to an end, so does the theory of idealism. Today it is actually passing out in sheer distress and idle motion. It is disappearing as that which is *subjective,* with lonely non-souls, with the vacuum of a world totally disparate to man and his knowledge. Such a theory is quite useful to capitalism because it is opposed to the militant optimism of revolution, and to the secular materialism of its theory—but this does not make it any more true. And idealism is vanishing in its *objective* guise inasmuch as it only conjures up or copies an epigonal Platonism, with a reification of logic, as in the case of Husserl, and indeed with mind as a demiurge, as though nothing had occurred since Aquinas or Hegel. This "objective" idealism also recommends itself to capitalism because the so-called *Gestalt* viewpoint deflects from any immaterial analysis. Moreover, the cult of spiritual values conceals the actual cult

132

of exchange values, which is capitalism. Hence the end of idealism offers a prospect which may be edifying but not felicitous, for the time is past when even dogs could be related to eternity. Even though this is true, indeed so obvious, any conclusions from this along the lines of vulgar Marxism must be avoided. Such an approach would be as erroneous as any total suspicion of ideology and is the counterpart of sociological schematization.

The rowdy controversialists of idealism do not discredit the old masters of idealism. Plato may owe something to Hegel but he owes no debt to the reactionary intellectual dwarfs of today. Idealism is a category, a very significant one, out of the actual history of philosophy, and therefore is not yet a completely exhausted mine. Eugen Dühring could treat the great idealists of the past with the ignorant impertinence suited to him, but Friedrich Engels honored the ancients precisely at his new location, having departed from them but continuing to learn from them. The ignorance of the bourgeoisie concerning Marx is not reciprocated in Marxism as ignorance concerning Socrates and Plato, or Nicholas of Cusa and Leibniz. Dialectics itself derives from idealistic modes of thought and lives in them first. It is from Hegel's philosophy that Marxism derives a great part of its superiority over the old unhistoric materialism of the natural-scientific kind, and Hegel is, among other things, a sort of *Summa* of the whole of idealistic philosophy. For this reason idealism must be studied, and in many ways must continue to be fertilized in a crypto-materialist sense; it must not be permitted to remain abstract or unknown.

Mere rightness of intent and a rapidly acquired schematism does not make a materialist summer. Of course, the eggshells of idealism must be swept away completely. But idealism also contains yolks and whatever else one may find. In short, the patrimony of knowledge from Plato to Plotinus, from Augustine to Occam, from Descartes to Hegel, demands the honor and attention it deserves after informed ideological criticism. For those who would master our ideological heritage, this should be as little beyond the scope of their knowledge as

133

Aeschylus or Dante, Shakespeare or Goethe. Indeed, for the young Marxist it is most important to gain acquaintance with the entire course of philosophy, with the gigantic stretch of idealism, and with the ferments working toward truth that are contained in the husks of idealism. To those who hastily dismiss it as though there were nothing left here to learn or think, one recommends Lenin's dictum: "A wise idealism is closer to a wise materialism than is a stupid materialism."

But I have already detained you too long with these introductory problems of philosophizing. Yet the relation between the university, Marxism, and philosophy must be considered to be very close and even immanent in certain respects. For our purposes, we may admit, with certain limitations, the liberal Professor Jaspers' definition: "The goal of the university is the disclosure of truth through the joint effort of investigators who are also teachers." This definition is only partly acceptable because it omits all reference to the people, to life in and with the struggling people and the people's front, without which the disclosure of truth becomes meaningless clap-trap, or the private sophistry of a world-fleeing spirit. The common endeavors of research workers and teachers require real *community.* The university, the *universitas literarum,* the institutional totality of the various sciences, is no more than a proficient, particularly resplendent expression of community—hence the origin of the original guild designation *universitas.* In the process a not insignificant role fell to philosophy, which has long felt itself to be the conscience of the university. It is the science in which the consciousness of the totality lives and has to live. Stemming from times when the progressive division of labor produced by capitalism, and then the increasing and almost anarchistic specialization of vocations, was still unknown, philosophy was concerned above all with the *unity* of knowledge. The common melody, the substantive coloration of all learning, is its particular concern and the essential aspect of its method and subject. When philosophy is doing its job, it offers that moving *cantus firmus* which provides stability and direction, in which and

134

about which the polyphony of knowledge moves. *Totum relucet in omnibus, omnia ubique* (the whole lights up again in all things; everything is everywhere), said Nicholas of Cusa in relation to Arabic philosophy; and both Leibniz and Hegel have made this same principle unforgettable.

Marxist philosophy must also fulfill its special obligation to make known the mighty voice of the *whither* and the *why*—the final voice without which unity grows torpid. The obligation is the same in regard to a necessary presence in the frontier problems: *philosophy stands on the front line,* knowledgeably active in the contemporary process of transformation, which is itself part of the world process. It stands there with the *new (novum),* a fundamental category which as yet has scarcely been investigated, and with *concrete utopia* as a determinant of objects and of reality.

For the world is quite other than finished. It is moving, and it is replete with dynamic tendency: that is, full of tension which undoubtedly results from the circumstance that something that is ready within the process of movement or of work is being impeded artificially. Marx defined this sort of tendency as a phenomenon artificially impeded, as a law impeded in its elaboration. The result is that it becomes an explosive trend, particularly when the environment has become crusted over, when the forms of life have become too tight for the dynamic and productive forces confined within them. Under such circumstances, the tension may be compared to a mass of over-heated gas which, as a consequence of such a social contradiction, will produce a mechanical explosion or an historical revolution.

Leibniz was the first to conceptualize and characterize "tendency" in a related sense—close to the concept of revolution and dialectical materialism insofar as he equated the greater space needed by a developed activity with the future. In a reply to Bayle in 1702, Leibniz noted that it was in accordance with this pattern that the present is pregnant with the future. There is a striking similarity here to Marx's declaration that force is the mid-wife of the coming society

135

with which the present one is pregnant. But tension and tendency, as the impetus of the revolution and the impetus toward liberation show, possess another quality. Unlike any other breakthrough, the socio-economic revolution produces not only "freedom from" but "freedom *to.*" The latter is indicated in both subjective and objective modes of expectation, as the *future* in revolutionary movements. This goal ahead is indicated in the *incipit vita nova* which filled the Peasants' Revolt, the French Revolution, and the Russian Revolution— albeit with varying content.

The tension in question is a tension directed *toward* something. Apart from, or rather *in* impeded necessity, it expresses the emergence or imminence of that necessity. Hence all critical points in the transition of a society from one stage to another are characterized by books of social expectation, dream landscapes of a better world, in short, social utopias. Augustine wrote *De Civitate Dei* in the transitional period from ancient to medieval-feudal society, Thomas More inaugurated a series of utopias in the bourgeois modern period, while Fourier marked the beginning of a trend to socialism as it became possible. All utopias, or nearly all, despite their feudal or bourgeois commission, predict communal ownership, in brief, have socialism in mind. To be sure, this is expressed in an abstract, imaginative manner, since the productive forces of the time were not ripe for socialism. Yet in all these utopias, these social voyages to Cytherea, there came to expression the expectant tendency that permeates all human history. Only in Marxism, however, did it find concrete expression, precisely because Marxism disclosed the real possibilities. And Marxism also reveals totality again—which is the method and the subject matter of all authentic philosophy. But for the first time this totality appears not as a *static,* as a *finished principle* of the whole, but rather as a *utopian,* or more precisely, as a *concrete utopian* totality, as the *process latency of a still unfinished world.*

Now it is this very *seriousness regarding the process of the totality* that makes Marxism the ineluctable orientation of philosophy, insofar as it is not just flea-snapping, or playing with sand castles far away from the truth. The process-seriousness of Marxism makes it, here too, the problem-and-answer area of every philosophy that is still possible. For it is the philosophical instrument for a farther-reaching, more comprehensive total knowledge of the really possible, which is implied in the reality apparent thus far. The *total reality* of the world has not yet completely emerged: it requires man, as the highest power of production and articulation, in order to find the "what" of its "so that," the real content of its thrust and drive. Indeed, the so-called "riddle of the world" consists not only of this, that the world—just the mere existence of it—is still a riddle to human reason, whereas in and for itself everything in it might be clear, ascertained and solved. Rather, the so-called riddle of the world is also an objectively real one, and the world itself an unsolved real problem in respect of its content. Something is not yet quite right in it; something in it is sick and calls for healing, for the transcendence of the proletariat, for the realization of philosophy, and for the realization of the proletariat and the transcendence of philosophy. And the process, with Marxism-and-philosophy as a special illumination, is the way of nature itself (of which we humans are a part) for the solution of the real problem, namely, the still outstanding objectivity that is in no way alien. There would be no process if the universe were already finished, if the world did not still need to be changed in the direction of knowability.

Certainly thought can push toward reality only when reality propels itself toward thought. Everything else is a sort of "putschism" of the concept, and hence necessarily condemned to abstraction, which grasps reality either by crawling empirically under it or by speculating, in utopian fashion, from above reality. But surely reality and the realism coordinated with it, this synonym of truth, is as such not yet finished. Hegel gave expression to the idea, to which he was by no means always faithful, that the truth is not a coin which is paid in cash and so can be pocketed, but that reality is a process. Only this process,

137

not the addition or mosaic of so-called facts, and hence of fixated processual factors, is reality, is represented in truth. Indeed, only this processual reality pushes at any given time toward thought, as it has to supply information regarding men and the rest of reality. The process itself, however, always has its "timetable" and a manifest *heliotropism*, being both capable of knowledge as well as requiring it. For this reason, in the authentic and responsible philosophy that we have to pursue, there is no *relativism* and certainly no *agnosticism*. No relativism, as though all cognitions were subjective or forever restricted to historical ideologies; and no agnosticism, as though *rerum natura*, the nature of things, were essentially uncognizable. Relativism and agnosticism are, rather, manifestations of cowardice or a decline of philosophy, and have no place in it.

Every resistance which the world presents to the courage to know and to the heroism to change is itself a step forward in dialectical-materialistic cognition, and a piece of the nothingness which must serve the totality best. Furthermore, the clumps or abysses in being, which is by no means smooth, are not simply irrational, or something semi-sacred and totally other, in the sense of superstition or of murderous shamanism. These elements present a task for human reason, for *creative humanism*, so that the excrescences are either destroyed in their nothingness, or, insofar as there is life there, so that life may be released and what is still irrational and locked up may be struck or broken open to the light. Consequently, depth is required—the opposite of flat exorcism or damned, blind talent. Reality itself is deep, precisely in that it is not yet locked up; and realism itself, when it is real, withdraws from the schema which knows everything in advance and construes everything according to formula. It is far truer that the timetable of the process is nowhere smooth and uninterrupted. It is not made up once and for all like some dull middle-class Cooks' tour where, on a mass basis, every last detail has already been tried out and rationally organized, so there is no discovery or hazard—everything having been predigested and disposed of. No *genuine future,* no understood historical trend, and no mastered historical necessity can be brought about in this way. On the contrary, adventure is in the vanguard of the dialectical-material process, together with a plethora of real problems which evoke courage in order to survive the venture, as well as penetratingly concrete reason—needed in order really to perceive the tendency. This wisdom, the always keen and well-thought-out, open and concrete wisdom of Lenin, watches over the path to the classless society. Out of this non-schematic approach new intermediate analyses of situations, always more concrete and expanded two-year, five-year, plans of theory and practice are always arising. They arise in the great plan of campaign which is socialist culture—necessary in order to reach the realm of freedom. But to this end all faces must be turned in one and the same direction: toward that rich multiverse of the one direction that is needed.

This is concept: dynamically informing, comprehending, and acting. As such, it does not remain colorless and inert, but takes in the whole range of truly human interest. As yet, there is interest without science and science without interest; this false separation must cease. The vocation of the new university is to carry out this task—as it hands on the old knowledge dynamically, permits the new that is ready to arise in a revolutionary way, and molds it appropriately for transmission ahead. In the freedom of this order, and in the order of this freedom, the centuries-old warfare between the spirit and the academy, between creation and the guild, has ceased. Also ceasing at last is the strife between the pulse beat and the syllogism. For the truth which does not comprehend trends and tendencies is no truth.

Now, materialistic dialectics—in the domain of human history—has as its real motive force both dissatisfaction and the hope that comes from unfulfilled need. In the times of reconstruction in which we stand, and of which we have to be effectively worthy, philosophy may characterize itself as *docta spes,* as *hope conceived in materialistic terms.* I shall close with the hope that between us there may be a double and yet a

139

single bond: that of trust and that which is known as the unity of transformative knowledge.

THE MARXIST CONCEPT
OF SCIENCE

Total purity of thought seems impossible. One can think clearly and consistently, perhaps, but without prejudice? Even in observation, and, of course, in the comprehension of what is observed, one man will get an idea that the other will not have at all, or only to a lesser extent—both still being at the pre-scientific level. Consequently, even in mere observation, and of course in judgment and evaluation, two people will scarcely have the same thing before them. The demand of research certainly objectifies matters to the degree that it may eliminate the purely accidental and individual differences. It seeks an observable world with objective and commonly observable characteristics, and freed as far as possible from such difference. To illustrate, the pulse of another is to be touched and measured not with one's thumb, but with the quiet index finger. Thus all personal sources of error and their sheer deception are to be eliminated.

But the elimination process does not extend to the group sources of error, in which various egos and their observational worlds are also embedded. What the group thinks appears

141

smoother, less personal, more general, and hence more objective; and if one group happens to be stronger than others, it wants to flatten out a weaker one intellectually, and frequently to absorb. Even in happier cases, thought does not emerge in a fashion so pure that it just rolls out, as it were, for it is always socially conditioned and frequently partisan. Hence the strong influence on thought and its process of observation was not even noticed until late.

In other words, partisanship is definitely operative here. There is no escaping it. This is useful to know, and a man can test his thinking from this perspective. It is usual in Marxism to acknowledge partisanship, if it be *intrinsic;* indeed, it has been made an intellectual key. Certainly the comfortable, the stupid, and windy careerists use it, always standing by the strongest guns *intra muros.* But, above all one can also note a narrow, unventilated and quite well-concealed partisanship *(extra muros)* when it is clearly nothing more than a purely acquisitive interest (and hence did and does not wish to acknowledge itself as such). This partisanship conceals its particular interest from the preponderant majority of the have-nots by diverting or mystifying strategies.

What is caught or imprisoned in the coils of partisanship must first be revealed in its class egotism, beneath its ideological ornaments and accessories, and its core must be disclosed as what it is—usually something far less attractive. Such insight into the reality of the matter was never very far from practical human knowledge. The shrewd saying that something is too good to be true already contains an admonition against self-deception and the world of illusions. And there are the related Freudian explanations of individuals' illusions on the basis of less flowery drives. We must not forget Schopenhauer, too, with his earlier reduction of the world to a single interest of the will. The reduction in Freud is made on the basis of individual psychology, whereas Schopenhauer's, on the contrary, is general and metaphysical.

But detection of partisanship grounded in interest above all requires, especially in regard to knowledge, the application of *social* analysis. What is central here is not libido (which very rarely produces history) nor any ahistorical personal will to live, but the interest in profit, and the master-servant relation in earlier relations of production and exchange, and the concealment thereof. Following this orientation and starting out from partisanship as exclusively class-egotistic enables one to employ an analytic method set forth by Marx as the economic interpretation of history. Marx's "theory of cognition" is expressed directly as follows: "The idea always compromises itself insofar as it is different from the interest." And: "The ruling ideas of any period are always the ideas of its ruling classes." This second statement expresses clearly the view that thought and science inevitably tend to support the class which is actually in a position of power or ready to assume it.

Marx's intention here has to be grasped in three aspects: a) the more critical-investigatory analysis within the political present; b) the more critical scrutiny of the *inheritable* past, above all the *cultural* tradition; c) only the *proletarian class* interest, in its unique partisanship, is both the *key* and the *lever* to the accomplishment of truth and justice. Straightforward partisanship—but for the science of *true* social consciousness and existence—became the *program*.

Point A. For the scales to fall from the eyes was and is surely more difficult as long as the self-victim still takes his own pretty words and exuberant speeches seriously, be they nationalistic or "universally humanistic," and apparently free of personal interest.

Now, counter to expectations, it will be more—not less—difficult for many to see through this, if the owner of false consciousness no longer has it personally, yet transmits it (the more subtly) to the servant who should have it. Every poor devil who carries his skin to market for the rich, be it even in the dirtiest war, knows how to sing his song about it—say, one about freedom and the armaments industry at the same time. There is hardly any difference, no more than an indication that a culmination is being reached, when the formulas employed are

143

leader and followers, woman's honor and high virtue, master race and salvation rune. To the unschooled, especially in the middle classes, this has appeared to be a delightfully bloody theater of their own; they have not recognized the profiteers behind it. This was the case, even though one does not have to dig very deeply in the marrow of honor to determine how much could be learned of the truth here.

Point B. It is clear, moreover, that, even if this is accomplished, we have only achieved part of the matter to be investigated. The economic interpretation of history, being comprehensive, looked also at the *more distant* past from which we have emerged—if only to find a *Mene Tekel.* For very often (and successfully) in the past, an X was written in place of a U, and a crusade was represented as what was wanted by God, when the god was really Mammon. So too when Marx (speaking more coldly than Mussolini or Gundolf, that purely poetic admirer of Caesar) says that the history of landed property is the true secret history of ancient Rome. Nevertheless, really great history, above all, cultural history, in Marx's economic-historic analysis does not only consist of matter for cold demythizing dissection. No, on the contrary, the economic factor and a totally class-interested partisanship may sometimes exert an historic effect as a midwife of more durable superstructures. In subsequent history these may serve quite a different "interest," even when (and indeed particularly when) the former economic basis has long since disappeared. Hence Marx says, in the Introduction to his *Critique of Political Economy* that *Greek art itself*—this erstwhile "superstructure" in a slave holding society (the interest of which can by no means be identified with human interest pure and simple)—is still regarded as immortal in every society (of any type), and indeed, "in certain respects, as a standard and insurpassable model." He makes a similar remark regarding the really "great ideas"—such as in regard to the illusionary notion of the *polis* in the French Revolution and its *"citoyen."* Here Marx sees not only disenchanting ideology, but notes that in the concept,

144

there inheres, notwithstanding all the contemporary illusions, a plethora of model ideas.

Accordingly, completely to debunk all the ideas that have appeared in history, dismissing them as mere false consciousness, or as the vertiginous reflex of economic class interests, is simple to misunderstand the economic interpretation of history in an inadequate, vulgar-Marxist way. To proceed in this manner is to obstruct insight into the role which, for Marx, the history of science plays in universal history; the more so since the sciences of a certain period, as the reflex or the aurora of an emerging new time and society, prepare the way ideologically for the economy of a society emerging in the future. One has only to think of the social-contract theory of classical natural law and of its influence on the much later American and French Revolution.

Nonetheless, the more culturally investigatory aspect of Marx's historical materialism also has a mist-dispelling function. By attributing an ideology to a particular economic interest, every drapery will be penetrated and removed. This applies not so much, or only, to the draperies of the historical Goebbels (which certainly exist, although hardly in a so completely cynical form) as to the highly idealistic draperies of idealistic historiography itself—"its deep feeling and high bombast" (as Jakob Burckhardt said). An almost purely idealistic historiography has survived to this day in the all too detached history of literature and of philosophy. It is possibly aiming too high (or too low) to require a modicum of economic historical theory in this kind of history—and, indeed, in all hermeneutics.

Cultural values, however hardy the cultural shoots, do not take root or reproduce, so to say, parthenogenetically, without a constant socio-economic mandate. The origins of the gigantic transformations in the world of the spirit from Zeuxis to Picasso, from Monteverdi to Schönberg, from Archimedes to Einstein, from Thales to Hegel, and so on, would otherwise be mysterious and at best an incestuous product of pure *spiritus*.

145

Instead, the socio-economic theory of culture maintains that, with changes in the infrastructure, corresponding changes occur in the superstructure (since Scheler, this has been known in the West as "the sociology of knowledge"). Consequently, even in matters of cultural luxury (where the pervasive suspicion of ideology does not apply), society exercises a determinative force according to the change in the class position of the party in question, and of partisanship. Indeed, this holds true at the very point where the distance between roof and foundation, that is, between the light of the spirit and economics, seems greatest. Take music for example: first comes the society of hierarchical estates and the fugue, and then there is bourgeois emancipated society and its dynamic sonata. Or, in philosophy, there is the ancient slave economy with contempt for work, and corresponding to it the interpretation of knowledge in Plato as predominantly "vision"; and then, by contrast, the bourgeois productive industrial society (*homo faber*), and the concept of knowledge in Kant, apprehended primarily as *production*. The fundamental difference between these concepts of knowledge was determined by economic and technological factors. Surely neither the musicians who went over to the dynamic sonata style, nor the very philosophers such as Hobbes, or even Kant, who interpreted cognition not as vision and representation but as the production of its subject matter, may have been aware of this partisanship or their "party affiliation." *But it was Hegel*—in this too (not a teacher of Marx for nothing)—who, because he recognized this connection with a particular social context, actually taught that every philosophy is its own "time" formulated in ideas.

Point C. It is not always hazardous, and surely not unconditionally so, to be so biased. This presupposes, of course, that there is no miserable mustiness or vestigial petty-bourgeois factor operative in the context, using people like animals. The same proviso extends to the other side of the ledger—that there is no socialist schematism which has become rotten, and which, as far as the red party is concerned, entails exhausted manoeuvers, clichés, and only dim readiness.

Not to be compared with this, however, is the sort of party involvement which prompts abandonment of what has not been ventilated in actuality or reflected upon in history. But, for Marx (as Lenin stresses), where there is such an *admitted* interest, it becomes *self-reflecting* "ideology." A thoroughgoing (constitutive) party consciousness, as is requisite— particularly in the Marxist concept of science—affords in this way an especially good conscience. To be sure, it has been (rather too generally) objected, even by a Marxist, that the standpoint of class consciousness does not permit of individual truth, does not tolerate a truth other than the universally valid varieties—which in fact feature no socialist interest. Thus Ernst Fischer (*Art and Coexistence,* 1960) did not include only treatment of any purely contemplative "truth in itself," but in justified rejection of censorious "slogan mongers" *a priori,* rejected any far too easy division of science into bourgeois or socialist; there are only "correct and false (or half-right, dubious) scientific findings." It might be objected here that Fischer overlooks the difference between the natural and the cultural sciences. The truth of Kepler's laws is of course independent of any class position on earth that exercises an apprehending and determinative effect; but it is a different matter with the truth regarding surplus value, the nature of commodities, and even the dependence of all the sciences themselves on their class infrastructure.

To be included here is a dictum of Lenin: "Were geometric axioms to contradict human interests, we would surely seek to confute them." Omitted here, at any rate, is Stalin's dictum, truly in the tradition of idealism, to the effect that not only language but also formal logic, mathematics, natural science, and technology are independent of any particular bases. Fischer was surely exaggerating when—for polemical reasons—he asserted that truths of the natural sciences and the cultural disciplines are virtually alike, not only in respect to

147

their discovery and recognition but in regard to their possessing a sort of possible truth in itself, free from any admixture of interest. Fischer is completely right here only insofar as his assertion is directed against the apparatus of an unventilated partisanship, of which the minor aspects may become interchanged with a party concern that is both world wide and open to the future. Of course, Marx taught that the party interest must be grounded in a truly revolutionary consciousness that would give it permanent direction in its world view, but he did not assert that this would preclude cultural coexistence or cultural inheritance from very different, and much earlier ideologies. Indeed, such a rejection of the cultural heritage would ultimately signify only that Marx's theory had been relativized to become a mere ideology of the working class and its party. Then it would be tied to a social locus, and would constitute not objective truth but only an exclusively proletarian *class truth,* in the same way that previously there had been exclusively bourgeois and feudal types, and so on.

To this extent Fischer is correct in rejecting mistaken Party standpoints in regard to the sciences, since these would not admit any knowledge other than some specially manufactured local proletarian variety. Ultimately, the proletarian class view would then become most narrow, least universal, and most impoverished spiritually in its world outlook—as has happened with some utter dilettantes. There would be no possible correspondence either with the "bourgeois" Einstein or with the semi-feudal Hegel. Marx criticized such slops of socialist party parochialism, but without denying the possibility of its universal right to claim that its knowledge might claim universality, as Fischer has done. As no one else, *Marx* sought to rescue and establish particularly and emphatically the universally valid truth of his social locus in the proletarian revolution, precisely in opposition to all previous class interests, that is, all previous ideologies, the preponderant number of which had to ideologize themselves.

For as Marx opined (despite all his isolation within the Party), the working class is the *only* one hitherto whose *very*

THE MARXIST CONCEPT OF SCIENCE

interest is not compatible with mystification and false consciousness whether subjective or objective, but only with a fully objective and universally valid analysis and examination of their condition. The purpose of this would, of course, be not to maintain or justify the condition so discovered, as had been done by all other ideologies hitherto, but precisely the reverse. For the first time, it was now the *interest* of a class itself to get to know its condition clearly, and so eliminate what for the proletariat was the most bitter aspect of universal self-alienation. Furthermore, the elimination of this self-alienation (that is, the reduction of all men, and even things, to commodities) was not to be confined to a self-emancipating proletariat, but as Marx taught, that very action would effect the emancipation of all mankind. We have now reached Point C. In the science of Marxism, the understanding of the proletarian class interest is to be at one and the same time the end and transformation of all class societies, and by definition, of the proletariat, the very last class as such.

The connection of a passionate involvement of this type with the restrained primacy of research may present many complications and it must be admitted that Marx did not fully think the matter through. There is presupposed here a harmony of the subjective will to emancipation, with an objectively real trend in history, with a dialectical open current of change. Of course, to the still widely diffused mechanistic type of materialism, this harmony is by no means self-evident, and indeed is regarded as having no place within it.

Nevertheless, Marxism maintains, precisely because of this very objective harmony of "putschism" within it, that it is quite radically different from the wretched partisanship of mere utilitarianism and pragmatism. This is why Lenin said, in this context, that Marxian socialism is omnipotent because it is true. This means that socialism wishes to be regarded as valid not because it is useful for those having an interest in its cause, but rather because it can be useful to them only because, to the degree, and in the measure that its interest is true, being the only one that comprehends contemporary social truth and is in

149

ON KARL MARX

alliance with it. To understand this remark of Lenin, it is always important that the thoroughgoing partisanship of Marxism should be one which is always indicated by critical analysis, and thoroughly oriented to practice. This is the case because Marxism, unlike anarchism, and even Sorel's anarcho-syndicalism, derives historically not only from Jacobin partisanship and its fist, but is an outgrowth of Hegelian philosophy reconsidered and inverted so that it stands right way up. Note that the intent here is as much that partisanship should become involved with thinking, as that thought itself should pursue truth (from the vantage point of revolutionary involvement) in the interest of a "world in the making," and not seek so-called "truth for its own sake." Only in such a context can action be thought too, and thought be useful action as well. A truth for its own sake, that is, in the sense of an investigation completely devoid of any interest, is thus impossible. Partisanship which has been "thought through" proceeds in this manner to the end, with the *vita activa* not supplanting the *vita contemplativa,* but going beyond it. Marx's most characteristic remark in this regard declares: "Philosophers have only *interpreted* the world in different ways; the point is to *change* it." This eleventh of Marx's Theses on Feuerbach is certainly not so strange to the *homo faber* of the new period, and it appears even less strange when a question is raised regarding the moral purpose of knowledge. As the last neo-Kantian, Emil Lask actually referred to "the primacy of practical reason even in logic." An inactive idolatry of purely contemplative theory alone cannot be the ultimate conclusion of wisdom—and certainly not wisdom itself. One has only to remember that a disregard of the practical consequences in the age of the atom bomb has involved criminal irresponsibility. The Marxist theory-practice had not only an epistemological but an ethical intention; in addition to possessing an epistemological orientation like early theories of this kind, Marxism was concerned not only with the *purpose* of science, but with the *scientific status* of purpose.

This approach, as already noted, is quite different from any atheoretical, merely utilitarian pragmatism, in that it demands and presupposes a more solid theoretical preparation and disposition to allow any durable, that is, concrete, action to be achieved. For Marxism, practical action, instead of being mere deceit and busy work, was to be so homogeneous with theory that, for Marx as for Engels, it represented the ultimately decisive proof of theory—in keeping with the adage that the proof of the pudding is in the eating.

Accordingly, by virtue of the contradictions that become apparent within it, action will lead to new theory in the interests of still newer action in the dialectical pattern. Hence there must be a continuing oscillation between theory and action, in contrast to every sort of dogmatic petrification of theory within itself.

Nevertheless, one thing is and remains certain—and this is appropriate in logic even as it accords with the doctrine of the primacy of practical reason: Marx does not hold that the idea of the true as that which is involved with action and even concretely useful, is the only criterion in the theory-praxis relationship.

On the contrary, he always clearly maintains (and this is central to his theory) that the useful has to validate itself not in a party affiliation that is class bound and isolated, but in one that is humanistic and ethical. The intent of socialist action, by its very definition *(per definitionem suam),* is not just to change the world, but to improve it supremely. Its vision is fixed upon the human race and the experiment of history, which is striving to move from the darkness into the light. All this would be for the most basic purpose, the publicly avowed ethical ultimate goal of this theory-practice relationship—the leap from the controlled realm of necessity to a realm of freedom yet to be liberated. This would occur because of, or despite, that remarkable perceptive dictum of Marx: "the revolution does not have to realize ideals but to set free existing tendencies. It has to do so in order to attain something which should protect

151

against the relativization of "all" ideologies: in short, what—as the advancement of the cause of an unalienated mankind—should be universally valid already.

The young Marx referred to this ultimate concept of the goal of theory-praxis only in general, yet quite unequivocally—for example: "To be radical is to grasp things by the root. But the root of all things is man." And, also in the Introduction to *A Critique of Hegel's Philosophy of Right,* there appears this newly formulated categorical imperative: "To topple all relationships in which man is a degraded, enslaved, abandoned, and contemptible creature." This goal clearly implies (as far as Marxism is concerned) a condemnation of the uneducated among its detractors as well as of the half-educated among its communicants. At the same time, it provides an immanent standard of criticism for its implementation (or nonimplementation) hitherto, especially in regard to "human material." Hence Marx's new version of the doctrine of man as the measure of all things *(homo mensura)* provides the most decisive criterion of party membership and partisanship, that doctrine which in the East is called "revisionism" and which in Marx's own concept of science is termed *real humanism* or *humane realism.*

EPICURUS AND KARL MARX

A man cannot be judged solely by the company he keeps. This is often true of young people, who are easily influenced. Indeed, even at a later age, the converse is sometimes true: that no man is responsible for his acquaintances. In true love, however, or in true friendship, the encounter is quite different: the relationship is essentially important for both parties, and characteristic of both. Moreover, an opinion, a doctrine, or a book can also become a friend—and in such cases it is irrelevant whether the bearer thereof is still living or long since dead. The person who meets with such a "friend," and who goes on with it of his own choice, shows quite clearly what he is, and even more, by the way he goes about things, what he may be capable of objectively. It is self-evident that any judgment on this score depends on the level of the material which so grips and concerns the individual, and its value is always, when it is worth speaking about, provisional.

Those who are satisfied only with ready-cooked nourishment are poor in spirit. A good cause, even if it is an old one, is always "in the making"; and if this be not understood, the cause will lose contact with life.

Wonder does not cease with knowledge—if it is unique and

153

does not vainly freshen everything it touches. Thus the person who is developing and therefore learning, apart from accumulating cognitive knowledge, ever and again comes upon some passage which grips him uniquely. It strikes and rouses the reader as though he had just met the original speaker of the passage as a living man. Thus such friends from the past assist, and continue to assist, the progress of one in the present.

How often the obvious is neglected, as a particularly instructive example will show. The young Marx, still thoroughly idealistic, but with materialism germinating in him, had come upon Epicurus. Hegel's treatment of him in his lectures had been predominantly devaluative, on the basis of Epicurus' alleged "arbitrariness" and even "tiresomeness." One reason for this negative criticism was Epicurus' concern with the "private," the sector to which even more than for the Stoics the Greek spirit was in withdrawal in his theory. But perhaps the more significant reason was Epicurus' atomic theory, the "inadequacy" of which Hegel had already stressed in his treatment of Leucippus and Democritus. The unique innovation of Epicurus, the free *swerving* of the atoms from the straight line, is touched on in just a few lines—but Hegel finds this quite "accidental" and hardly interesting.

In his dissertation on *The Difference between the Democritean and Epicurean Philosophies of Nature,* Marx was eagerly aroused by this very point. He does indeed accept Hegel's minus sign in regard to the "private" doctrine taught by Epicurus (and the Stoics)—but also accepts "the good fortune included in such misfortune," namely, the "subjective form"—as the acquisition of self-consciousness in the philosopher's attitude toward the world. For Marx, then still a young Hegelian, Epicurus became, *for this reason,* the most significant representative of enlightenment in antiquity. But what is decisive is the interest, attention, detail, and evaluation Marx devotes in particular to Epicurus' *doctrine of a swerve in the fall of the atoms,* and the cosmogonic innovation therein. Here Marx detects a contact with his own "innovations" in opposition to mechanism and fatalism. Hence he stresses the signifi-

154

cance of a deviation of the falling atoms from the vertical fall line, whereby they alone are able to collide with one another obliquely as well. Only in this way, Epicurus had said, was it possible for atom complexes and hence bodies, and above all the vortex formations of their movements, to arise; otherwise, everything would be a merely parallel "persistent rain of atoms" (Lucretius). Of course, once the world of bodies with its many "vortices" and directions had arisen, the relative "freedom" of a purely parallel course was abrogated. Yet it survives in the freedom of choice and the ethical self-determination of human "atoms," of individuals. Of course, the parallel falling movement of the atoms, from which the swerve or *"clinamen"* is made, is found only in Epicurus and not in Democritus. The latter had taught not only an atomic motion of the falling variety in all directions, but one that was always without any possible "choice" of a change, inviolably and firmly controlled by the purely mechanical "necessity" of its event, as was the case with all others. Here Epicurus opposed what seemed to be wholly mechanistic, indeed a total fatalism, in Democritus. Epicurus offered a starting point against at least a purely mechanical determinism completely alien to the subject. Said Marx in his dissertation: "In Epicurus, therefore, atomism, with all its contradictions, as the natural science of self-consciousness, which is an absolute principle unto itself under the form of abstract uniqueness, has been taken to the extreme conclusion, which is its dissolution and conscious opposition to the universal. For Democritus, on the contrary, the atom is only the universal objective expression of the empirical investigation of nature in general" (MEGA, I, 1/1, p. 52). Accordingly, as Marx notes, Democritus confirmed only the existence of atoms, while Epicurus introduced the principle of the "effective beginning," the "energizing principle" which allows it, *ab ovo,* to influence any mere external pressure and weight. This is the "difference between Epicurus and Democritus," as emphasized by Marx.

To be sure, Marx himself vigorously rejected the merely private occurrence of this "subjective factor" in Epicurus'

155

ethics as an asocial atomism, insofar as this behavior isolated men and plainly made them unfit for any *active* influence upon the environing world. Withdrawal from the world helps neither men nor their own being in existence. "Abstract uniqueness is freedom from existence, not freedom in existence, and is unable to bring illumination to the light of being." Yet while Marx thus rejects Epicurus' "ataraxy" as a mere symptom of the declining Greek *polis,* the dissertation stresses all the more the energy of a "free will" which Marx obtained from Epicurus' countermove—notwithstanding his mistaken isolation of freedom as mere abstract individuality in the "lamplight of privacy," as a result of which freedom does not come into its full essence. Yet because of the correct preservation of the swerve and of its background, although still in spiritualized wrapping, the dialectical interplay of the subjective and objective factors is evident in the dissertation. The fact that the individual implements his freedom in turning toward the world and not in any abstract, isolated turning away from it, brings "the philosophical idea into the world"—as something to be altered and as something alterable. Of course, Marx's dissertation still retains many traces of young Hegelian idealism, including the "natural science of self-consciousness" that Marx found in Epicurus' atomism, as well as vestiges of Bruno Bauer's *Philosophy of Self-Consciousness,* and the opinion that the course of history, the "purification of reality," could be executed by philosophy alone, if "critical." Yet there is another note altogether characteristic of the young Marx: the First and Eleventh Theses on Feuerbach are already present *in statu nascendi* in the references to Epicurus.

The very first thesis also reproaches earlier materialism for understanding perception "only in the form of objects" and not as "sensuous human activity, praxis, not subjectively." As for the Eleventh Thesis, with its emphasis on inducing practical changes in Feuerbach's world, "the energizing principle," with its orientation to dynamic declination and not mere mechanical inclination, already features the impetus of this thesis: that is, that the world must be changed.

156

The power of the atom to swerve soon showed that Epicurus was in the right; it also stood in opposition to the first automatic schema, which impeded the world still in the process of arising. In order to emerge from the mere "rain of atoms" (Lucretius), the world requires more than the parallel movement of its atoms. Epicurus could already summon that important subjective factor *(facultas agendi)* into his purview even though the important objective factor (law, *norma agendi)* was not yet quite complete. *In nuce,* then, Democritus is read through Epicurus: or necessity *(ananke)* is transformed from the status of an interdict, and becomes a really world-constructive order. No one was interested in what the young Marx was writing at the time of his dissertation. But as far as Epicurus was concerned it was not long before some cursory notice, at least, was taken of his remarkable atomic "swerve." In 1897, one Goedeckemeyer "again" treated this theme in a dissertation, and unwittingly employed a similar title: *Epicurus' Relationship to Democritus in the Philosophy of Nature.* In 1907, H. Gomperz, the learned historian of philosophy, had a patronizing word to say for the same ancient curiosity— though on questionable grounds. In his *The Problem of Free Will* (1907), he sees in "this otherwise generally despised velleity of Epicurus" a deeper and more justified idea, since it might well be the principle of the so-called "theory of spontaneity."

As it happened, a later, quite literal, and so completely perverse reaction was yet to come—the *curiosum* was to become a sensation. It transcended the limited range of interested readers, not because Heisenberg's principle of indeterminacy became so important in physics and really caused people to remember Epicurus' speculative swirls, but because, almost at the same time, anti-Marxist interests readily greeted anti-reason *(irratio)* and anti-nomianism, even when these were only apparently so, and extended them to society.

The uncertainty principle taught among other things that the observation of subatomic processes indicates no strongly determined causal nexus, but only a statistically probable

157

consequence. Hence a factor of uncertainty in mere observation (influence of the light employed to measure the space or the velocity of atoms), and on the other hand an element of uncertainty in the wave-corpuscle relation of the atom itself, flow into one another. In any case, precisely the strict regularity of nature, the erstwhile darling, was broken. But this also seemed to injure the *total* commitment to law of Marxism. Late bourgeois economics had long been interested in producing just such an injury. For even though it itself became increasingly rationalized, it was greatly concerned, for obvious reasons, to portray the course of social life as a whole as not objectively characterized by lawful behavior. Dilthey's mimpathizing "understanding" (in psychology and the historical sciences), instead of merely analytical and causal "explanation" (in the natural sciences), had begun this campaign against the idea of lawfulness. The so-called "philosophy of life" in Bergson and beyond stated that the distinctive glory of its *élan vital* was that it was constantly changing its direction like a graph. Here too, one detects a *perversion* of the *clinamen.* Under fascism, this tendency continued from stage to stage: in Gentile there is only the *"atto puro"* to begin with—one that (as the Duce) can do what it wishes with objective determinations and laws; and *as the Duce* means with the full excess of accident—as the *grande animatore.* Yet even this is only the ultimate consequence of the ideological campaign against the "logic of history," and against its timetable and, indeed, all cosmic laws. This was the unfortunate perverse course taken by the late recognition of ³picurus' cuckoo egg, which he alone had laid in the nest of rigid mechanistics. All the more significant, then, is the young Marx's fascination by the matter. Here the "subjective factor" is no fetish and no mere external mechanical necessity. A true evaluation of living forces (here the subjective factors) never occurs without a true evaluation of determination by the factors of objective conditioning in which the subjective element can alone develop—and, O Epicurus, vice versa, in mutuality.

158

UPRIGHT CARRIAGE,
CONCRETE UTOPIA

1.

What you don't know can't hurt you. Thus the lukewarm and indifferent in regard to Marx; they enjoy, even now, the stupidity of their actions. The outspoken enemies, the Nazis, certainly knew nothing at all—except lies, which is very much worse. The outcome was madness—a madness not only of hurt but of anguish, and ultimately of the license to kill.

2.

But how were (and are) the ignorant to be given knowledge? How are the striving and ferment of socialism to be kept alive in the young people of the Western world? And, of course, there are the young people of the Eastern bloc; they are not in ferment, but they are critically oriented, and their minds are inspired by a Marx other than the Marx of the apparatchiks— who have no minds at all. In the West, knowledge of Marx, or even curiosity regarding him, is still significantly inadequate, one-dimensional, or obviously distorted.

How different it seemed in the Twenties, when the abortive revolutions of 1918 had not been forgotten and the Soviet Union was still effectively pre-Stalinist. At that time (in Germany, at least) a knowledge of the fundamental concepts of Marxism was almost a test of a student's intelligence—not only in the universities of Heidelberg and Frankfurt. But Hitler came to power: not only among the petite bourgeoisie and the leading capitalists (who greeted him as a saviour when they themselves had summoned him against the Red front). One of the main reasons for this, apart from Social Democratic spiritlessness and Imperial nostalgia, was the almost wholly false language of Communist propaganda. Offering paper fanaticism and sectarian evangelism, they left the entire field of "opposition" to the "system" by the peasantry and the petite bourgeoisie, to the Fascist snarl and roar, to deception and misuse. In spite of these lessons, and in spite of the defeat and destruction of the arch-enemy, Nazism, the attempt to evoke an adequate interest in Marxism among the ordinary people in the West has met with hardly any success.

3.

The "new start" that was a possibility after Hitler never really came to pass, despite frequent use of the slogan. In West Germany, the Eastern image was almost totally ineffectual. The postwar "economic miracle" in the Federal Republic had an especially palliative effect, the more so as it was completely unexpected after the defeat, and certainly did not accord with the Marxist thesis of the disintegration of an economy based on profit. The right-wing Social Democrats, therefore, continued to propose the "throwing off of ballast," even though ever since 1914 they had not previously been so emphatic about that. After 1919, Marxism was increasingly reduced to a theory of reform, and lost its acute dynamic tension and sharpness; it was consciously adapted to the bourgeois economy, the class struggle was relaxed to the point

160

of elimination, and the dialectics of revolution was discarded. All this destroyed Marxist enthusiasm and concern in broad areas of the population, especially among the young; all the more so because the newly established Communist party, in the wake of Lenin, set itself up as the home of genuine Marxism—which it abandoned under Stalin, with the result that the former party of Bebel and Rosa Luxemburg, in terms of Marxist theory as well, hardly existed or exerted any appeal. Interest in Marx among all non-Communists was weakened and watered down; eventually the complete lack of interest so strongly desired by the ruling class was effected by Stalinism. Indeed, this lack of appeal was increased by an emotional antagonism—still prevalent in regard to its original stimulus. Of course, all those in the West who permitted and still condone the existence of slums, who willingly served the master race and the bestiality of Hitlerism, and even the erstwhile judges of Nuremberg who brought about the hell of Vietnam have no right in this regard to criticize Stalinism, or at least Stalin as a bloody tyrant. Nevertheless, Marxism, about which really nothing was known, was immeasurably discredited by Stalin's terror, which was all people knew of at the time. Unfortunately, this devaluation of Marxism was apparent not only among the ignorant but among the neutral, the young, and the hopeful. Even Togliatti, pure, wise, and blameless, was brought to ask: "Is it the fault of the system?"—to ask if there was something peculiarly Marxist in the system which permitted, made possible, or at least did not hinder such a development. Space for genuine Marxist propaganda against the anti-propaganda of Stalinism was not long available in the Polish or Hungarian "spring" of October 1956; nor did this space coincide (as was the case with the authentic "spring" in Czechoslovakia) with the young revolutionary movements in the West. Stalinist anti-Marxist propaganda continued its work in the West, delaying conversion to the authentic Marx, as when an East German radio official declared and threatened in 1968, apropos of the "spring" in Prague: "In a truly Socialist state, there are no contrary voices to be heard; the only

161

dialogue with the opposition takes place in the courtroom." In the West there could be only possible reaction to such expressions of "Marxism" (the opponents of Marxism could scarcely manage a more damaging image themselves): that Marxism is interchangeable with Nazism, and that a state of affairs in which we are protected from that kind of Marx is something devoutly to be wished.

As the above quotation shows, Marxism suffers not so much from its enemies as from its alleged friends. The hardly attractive, even negative, propaganda power of the East (to a great extent taken up by its own internal difficulties) is, at least primarily, the result of the unexpected victory of Marxism not in the bourgeois democratic West, as Marx had always assumed, but in the Czarist East. The purely economic backwardness of the old Russia (even though still evident today in an apparently inadequate satisfaction of consumer needs) is far less important here than the particular despotism which, for the West, is the face of the success-in-action of Soviet Marxism. This, of course, is a source of joy to Wall Street and the equivalents of the Springer publishing concern. But it is a problem and a stumbling block for the Marxism whose inception has always proclaimed the necessity of a leap from the realm of necessity into that of freedom.

4.

It must never be forgotten that the Red birth occurred in Russia. The ten days that shook the world started at the Neva, and nowhere else. Russia was the weakest link in the chain and hence the one that would break most readily and first, but it was primarily the masses and their leader who destroyed it. Marx had considered the moujik to be the last possible candidate for the Red soldiery, even though nineteenth-century Russia had been shaken by uprisings ever since the Decembrists, and the frequent explosions of the bomb of anarchism. Yet Napoleon's prophecy has come true: "In a

hundred years Europe will be either Republican or Cossack."
The final outcome was that primarily the defeated Russian
Army, not the defeated German Army (from which Lenin still
expected everything), carried Marx in its knapsack. Nevertheless, the change in the timetable of the Revolution, with Russia
suddenly the first subject, brought about problems. The difficulties were certainly masterfully reduced by Lenin's call for
electrification plus Socialism. Indeed, until long into Stalin's
regime, Marxism was at home only in the Soviet Union, the
very place that was apparently so ill-equipped to accommodate
it. This lasted until the infusions of Czarism into Soviet
Marxism became more obvious, and indeed began to tarnish
the image of Marxism itself, until the all too widely asked
question (objectively comprehensible only among true Marxists) arose: Had Marxism changed out of all recognition under
Stalinism, or was its real nature even more recognizable in
certain regards?

But of course this question should be addressed not to Marx
but to the Russian State Church. The essential must be
distinguished from the inessential; the time question is very
important: the start was made not in the more developed
bourgeois countries where there was at least a formal democracy. If we are to understand other difficulties in Soviet
Marxism which derive from the abnormal timetable and are
conditioned by local suasions, we have both to examine the
first Socialist experiment quite fairly, and to exhibit the
sobriety, scientific validity, and luminosity of Marxism in
itself. It should be clear that the absence of bourgeois revolutionary modernization in Czarist Russia necessarily had specific consequences in the new Russia. There the springs of
social wealth ran not richer but poorer than in more developed
capitalist countries. In the absence of long-standing forms of
bourgeois freedom the predicted dictatorship of the proletariat
had to be established directly on the basis of the Czarism that
had immediately preceded it. Among the results were the
personality cult, an extensive and absolutist centralization,
lack of room for any except a "criminal" opposition, the terror

163

and the police state, and an all-powerful state police—even when complete security for the Socialist power had been won internally. In short, besides many excellent Marxist achievements, a wholly undemocratic "Socialism" was established on the historical basis of Russian reaction. Accordingly, enslavement in practice has to be rigorously distinguished from the *real* problems of the revision of Marxism: they are not among the fruits that grow out of it alone. Of course, it is pertinent to ask why certain purely theoretical features in Marx did not hinder the emergence of such practices, even if they did not evoke them. For example, why was the dictatorship of the proletariat not so rigorously conceived from the outset that Stalinism could not change it into a dictatorship over the proletariat? Again, what connection was there between the slight, imprecise or even precise neo-classicism of Marxist aesthetics and the dictatorship of utterly uncreative functionaries over artists and writers that could so affect the evolution of Soviet art?

But all this does not allow us firmly to conclude that pre-Soviet theory contains premises corresponding to backward and so often wretched actions, even though the central Marxist concept of the relationship between theory and practice would allow us to judge and to know by the fruits of human actions. To a considerable extent, the reactionary conditions prevalent before and after 1918 enable us to understand how the opposite of the predicted "withering away of the State" could occur, even though they do not help us to forgive it. This "withering away" is clearly an inviolable central part of Marxist thought, which otherwise has very few perspectives on the future. Marx indicated three sources of his theory: English economics, the French Revolution (and utopia), and German classical philosophy. For obvious reasons, the East was not included. Indeed, Marx concluded his Introduction to *A Critique of Hegel's Philosophy of Right* with the following (unfulfilled) prophecy: "When all the inner conditions [for the victory of the working class] are ripe, the day of German resurrection will be announced by the crowing of the French rooster." A prophecy that has not been real-ized—yet it will come true in the future if taken as referring to a storming of all the Bastilles in the world.

5.

The stimuli of radical socialism are still effective. The genuine-ly Marxist insights have demonstrated their staying power, and they will endure until they have been put into action and realized. The revolutionary youth of today are again learning with amazing readiness and speed (too speedily, in some cases) and will no longer tolerate contradiction. Their learning and agitation are anarchistic to a significant extent when they incline more to Bakunin than to Marx. The direction of Bakunin's teaching was primarily opposition to the oppressive State rather than to an exploitative economic system, as though the exploitation derived essentially from the subjuga-tion, and the State alone was the basis of evil. Yet even this shift in the orientation of the revolutionary struggle does not signify a new polemic against the original Marx, and, indeed, might more readily be directed against the Stalinism which claims to be descended from Marx. With regard to the enduring content of Marxist fundamentals, it is significant that not Bakunin but the Marxist Trotsky is cited by the anti-Stalinist movement. The anti-Establishment declarations from Berkeley to Warsaw (and Moscow) contain Bakuninisms that are far from anti-Marxist, being directed against tyranny everywhere (indeed the formation of "councils" and Soviets was originally an anarchist idea). Authentic Marxism, which always possesses the potentiality of further development, displays the retrograde features wished upon it by reaction-aries and (alas!) the *erstwhile* Social Democrats, only when it is inauthentic and has ceased to evolve. Other reactionary ele-ments—those held fast by dogmatic formulas—are rendered ineffectual by the catechism of a Marxism contrary to Marx, in which he appears almost as the patron saint of sterility.

165

Informed analysis, not sterility, is the dynamic characteristic of all the fundamental propositions of Marxism, and remains necessary and valid inasmuch as, since Marx, the essential nature of capitalism has not changed, and re-establishes itself time and again.

Admittedly, since his time some manifestations of the essential nature of capitalism have changed as it has branched out in new directions. Hence the theory of the progressive impoverishment of the proletariat in highly developed capitalist countries (a theory of major importance when Marx and Engels were alive) is now no longer valid—or at least its validity is suspended until a fresh crisis hits the employed much harder than the big employers, and the fashionable slogan of the "social partnership" is discarded. But in fact the Negroes of North America, the Indios and others in Latin America, and the hungry masses of India can hardly be said to have experienced the invalidity of the theory of impoverishment, and this basic Marxist proposition has been outdated only in white countries with an economic boom, where the very circumstances of its non-applicability make it worthy of regard.

On the other hand, certain elements of original Marxism remain wholly valid: its thorough investigatory and analytic pursuit of the knowledge of social realities; its dialectics of the contradictions which tend toward a socialist transformation; and those quintessential insights of Marxism relating to class structures as a whole and in detail. The contradictions within capitalism, as the most developed of these structures, enable us to perceive most clearly the totality of alienation and self-alienation. Other noteworthy elements are the appreciation of labor as the sole source of value; of the distribution of surplus value, the largest portion of which goes to the entrepreneurs, leaving the worker only as much as he needs to maintain his labor power. Another insight is that in a commodity society the only value that the proletarian possesses is the labor power he has to sell, and that in general such a society represents the transformation of all human beings into

166

commodities. This is tantamount to a reification, a total self-alienation, even of the capitalists themselves (with the one difference that these feel at their ease in such a state); and even to an alienation of things which have been taken into the circulation of commodities, and the deception of a fate independent of men and not comprehended in truth. And the truth is that in the alienated product, and in the process which apparently takes place automatically behind our backs and over our heads, man the producer has been forgotten together with the particular relations of production which primarily go to make up the more or less numinously effective "spirit" of a society.

Another noteworthy insight of Marx relates to the economico-technical, materially evident basis or infrastructure, which determines not only the *political and social* superstructure ("handmills conditioned the nature of the feudal society, whereas the steam mill determined that of capitalist society"), but the context of any particular *cultural* superstructure. Here Marx, in contrast to subsequent popularizers and simplifiers of his theories, rarely forgot the intermediate links between "economy" and "ideology." But even then he opposed the pure idealists, and the fetishists of "spirit," by ensuring that any examination of, say, classical antiquity or the Gothic and Baroque periods took into account the socio-economic conditions which made such phenomena possible in the first place. Since then, a so-called "sociology of culture" has come into being, even in bourgeois circles. In any case, the superstition that cultural epochs and their works of art succeed one another wholly by means of a sort of incest or even parthenogenesis has been severely curtailed. The realization of the priority of the economic basis provided, in regard to the totality of history, the most influential and essentially dialectical insight that the particular dominant spirit of an age is not only the spirit of its particular dominant class, but the movement of history in aggregate as the history of a movement of classes or of a class dialectics, that is, the contradiction that arises within every ruling class by reason of the maturation of the subsequent class and society. This process will persist as long as we must wait until the condemned of this earth finally eliminate every class society and the mere prehistory of man to date, together with the enduring and inhuman scandal of a division of mankind into masters and slaves. First and last, this struggle demands full solidarity with the weary and the heavy-laden: "The supersession of the proletariat is the fulfillment of philosophy."

The ultimate, enduring insight of Marx is that truth does not exist for its own sake but implies emancipation, and an interpretation of the world which has the transformation of the world as its goal and meaning, providing a key in theory and leverage in practice. Whoever finds this orientation of philosophical theory to humanistic practice (and to nothing else) superannuated is a supporter of things as they are for whom little can be done. Essential Marxism contains in its past so much that is future still unfulfilled: it is as if everything that it intends under world improvement were still ahead of us even in our world of alluring achievements. But of course, in accordance with the Marxist theory of the maturation of history, remote from all abstract utopian outlines. Yet not, as Marx himself thought, requiring the absence of any utopia at all; for what lies before us is the beginning of that which cannot grow old and cannot be outdated—the beginning of the way to the actual, the *concrete* utopia.

6.

We must never forget the importance of man's upright carriage—the proper stature that he has not yet achieved—in the traditional uplifting sense postulated by the theoreticians of natural law. It was Engels who described the great social utopias, especially those of Fourier, Owen, and St. Simon, as precursors of Socialism. On the other hand, the classical natural law of the seventeenth and eighteenth centuries, which

168

was oriented not so much to human happiness as to human dignity, was found less worthy of note, even though it had given an essential ideological impetus to the English, American, and French Revolutions; and even though the slogan Freedom, Equality, and Fraternity is certainly concerned more with "wrongs" than with a happy island and a corresponding social vision. Moreover, the dignity of the human individual (in whom, as Kant said, mankind is to be honored) was not, or at least was not primarily, a Marxist slogan of emancipation. There are few spokesmen for natural law among the precursors of socialism, despite significant references by Marx and Engels to individual qualities, the socialist emancipation of all individuals, the end of control over persons, and the withering away of the State. Undoubtedly, there is in Marx a certain lack of emphasis on, and sometimes also an absence of, enlightenment, which certainly served to reinforce the centralizing tendency in Stalinism, which arose from the previous absence in Russia of any achievement of bourgeois liberation. In addition, hindsight shows that the comparatively weak emphasis on personal freedoms in Marx corresponded to his rejection of all terms of entrepreneurial ideology, of its *laissez-faire, laissez-aller* individual economic interests which helped to produce and did not merely accompany, classic natural law theory. The exclusion of natural law and its eminently humanistic concern (by no means restricted to private enterprise) from Marxism was probably assisted by the bourgeois decline of the theory, at first in the Romantic-historicist and then in the legal-positivist jurisprudence of the nineteenth century. Certainly, Rosa Luxemburg's "No socialism without democracy!" (that is, without the enfranchisement of socialist individuals) is deeply indebted to the other precursors of socialism, and represents a heritage which, in general, has not been sufficiently drawn upon. The realization of this inheritance, of a no longer bourgeois but socialist emancipation, will be the decisive factor in the future with regard to the countenance of freedom within communism. The orthopedics of the upright posture is one of its most pressing obligations, and none other than humanistic socialism features it as the supreme human right.

7.

Finally, Marx is consciously and intentionally sparing of color in depicting the possible future. In this respect he properly parts company with his utopian predecessors, who all too often posited their mere wishes as the actuality of the future, engendered in the mind and produced in the form of utopian "novels" which had little or no impact on the course of social life. Of course, even this still abstract activity was seldom wholly private and independent of circumambient reality: in general, the successive utopias were not only attached, but in some cases appropriate, to their particular age. Hence, Sir Thomas More was an English "liberal," Campanella with his "solar State" corresponded to the contemporary absolutisms of Spain and France, while St. Simon, two hundred years later, offered the magical formula *"l'industrie."* Yet an unmediated element, that is, unmediated with the existing reality, and merely introduced from outside to be set against the trends of the present reality, even here endowed the grand projections and forecasts of the utopias with the strain of dream content which the Philistine calls pious superstition, and which until very recently made all utopian constructions seem windy. Marx went on to produce instead extremely precise economic analyses regarding commodities and their circulation. In *Capital* he carried out an analytical demystification by means of economics, and offered the weary and heavy-laden a mediation of the subjective with the objectively real contradictions in their actual conditions, thus providing them with real assistance in the shape of an economic interpretation of history and historico-dialectical materialism. Having rejected the term "utopia," he proficiently restricted the immediate perspective to the next step to the goal. But the goal itself was to have and maintain the immanent goal of the "transformation of the

170

realm of necessity into that of freedom." And even though this is still not in sight, not a tangible reality, due space has been provided for its appearance in the future: one might say that Marx was a scientific iconoclast who prepared the way for the commonwealth of freedom. Nevertheless, the advance from utopia to science was too extreme, as if everything utopian were purely abstract or even illusionary, and as if science were concerned only with facts—a far cry from Marx the process thinker, the progress thinker. A Marxism that has turned into a wholly empiricist methodology is wrong in cancelling two essential utopian elements, which ultimately lead into the realm of truth—first, *ideals*, and, secondly, all ultimate *utopica*—is wrong in discarding them as forever bound to remain without concrete realization. Both ideals and utopian ends are essential components of Marxism now, and most certainly in the future. Not only political economy but the tendency toward and the latency of an ultimate are effective, and actually effective, in Marxism.

8.

It is supremely important that the committed and the aware should dream ahead, as the new requires. Lenin himself said precisely this—shocking many, but not young people, without whom no socialist movement could endure. Thus Lenin, by no means an abstract utopian: "What do we have to dream about? . . . I shall go further, and ask whether a Marxist has actually any right to dream if he remembers that mankind after Marx must always set itself only the tasks that it can carry out . . . Yet if men were totally unable to dream . . . they would be quite unable to foreglimpse in the imagination, as a unified and completed picture, the work which is just beginning to take shape in their hands . . . and I really cannot think what motive would persuade them to undertake extensive and arduous labors in the realms of art, science, and practical life, and to complete them." Such is the opinion of Lenin, and of some of

171

the authorities he uses—ironically—to put forward his ideas. Ideal images, insofar as they are not exclusively subjective, quite legitimately—as the subjective ideal tendency—hasten ahead of and precede an objective historical tendency, which need not necessarily rush ahead to meet its precursory dreams.

Admittedly, in contradistinction to all merely subjective and rhetorical moralizing, Marx stressed the fact that the revolutionary working class did not have to realize any ideals, but only to liberate the existing social tendencies (of which society is now full). Yet people will neither die for, nor enthuse over, a well-designed production plan alone. And, on the other hand, it was not just the inadequate evolution of material prosperity that induced near-indifference in both proletariat and intelligentsia in the East, but the mean and contrary method of accomplishing socialist ideals—the "real humanism" which Marx had expressly worked for.

Real humanism is entirely synonymous, in regard to what *is* mediated in accordance with its proper tendency, *and* its latent, still ideal content, with *concrete utopia*—that paradox for all empiricists which first arose and, indeed, became a possibility, in the Twenties. Actual utopia is an apparent contradiction *in adjecto,* and was all too soon taken all too lightly; it signifies that utopian possibilities are established in the concreteness and openness of the material of history: indeed, of the material of nature itself. This is the objective-real possibility which surrounds existing actuality with tremendous latency, and affords the potency of *human* hope its link with the *potentiality within the world.* Concrete utopia is bound up with dialectical materialism, and prevents it from defaulting—prevents it from discarding its visions of a goal ahead and gives it the *novum* of a dialectical-*utopian* materialism. This is a wide field occupied by matter itself, as a "being-in-possibility," as a potentiality pregnant with new though distant modes of life—leading to the "naturalization of man" and the "humanization of nature," as Marx, implicitly refuting any denial of far-distant objectives, put it in the *Economic and Philosophic Manuscripts.*

172

The inhumanity of our world certainly has many reasons to fear the final celebration of Marxism, and the cancellation, once and for all, of any bondage—of any master-slave relationship. Right and justice, freed from mere rhetoric and restrictive formularies, must show the fruits of emancipation from acquisition of a morality without enslavement, of an art without faith in sheer illusion and superstition. In 1968 we celebrated the one hundred and fiftieth anniversary of the birth of Karl Marx. We still have reason to hope for a *concrete* celebration in 2018, and not one that coincides with Negro riots, starvation in India, and neo-fascism.

Prometheus, said the young Marx, is really the most illustrious saint in the philosophical calendar. The profound meaning of this statement is something that will never again be pinned to the rocks or nailed to the cross. On the contrary, it is that which is yet to be shown forth: *quod erit demonstrandum.*

DATE DUE

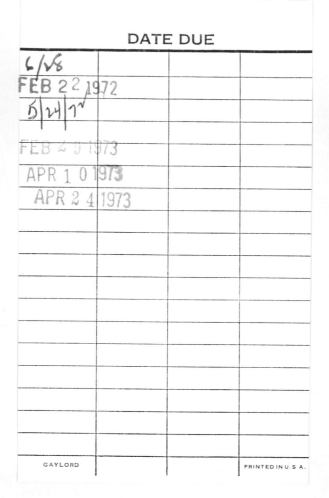

6/√8			
FEB 22 1972			
5/24/7			
FEB 4 9 1973			
APR 1 0 1973			
APR 2 4 1973			
GAYLORD			PRINTED IN U.S.A.